# MEDIEVAL MYSTICISM OF INDIA

# MEDIEVAL MYSTICISM OF INDIA

KSHITIMOHAN SEN

GYAN

*Published by*

Gyan Publishing House
5, Ansari Road
Daryaganj, New Delhi-110002
Phone: 011-47034999, 9811692060
E-mail: books@gyanbooks.com

*Distribution Network*
gyanbooks.com
India, USA, Canada, UK, Australia



ISBN: 978-93-7097-632-0 (PB)

First Published, 1908

2nd Impression 2025

*Printed at:* Gyan Press, Delhi.



**MEDIEVAL MYSTICISM OF INDIA**
Author: KSHITIMOHAN SEN

# MEDIEVAL MYSTICISM OF INDIA

*by*

KSHITIMOHAN SEN

*With a Foreword by*

RABINDRANATH TAGORE

*Authorized Translation*
*from the Bengali*
*by*
MANOMOHAN GHOSH

To

ALL THOSE

Who have felt the Supreme Spirit
in rare moments of self-realization

and

Who seek life's fulfilment in a love
that transcends limitations of creeds,
customs and of race,

I humbly dedicate this effort of mine.

K. S.

# FOREWORD

Text books of Indian History, which we read, deal mostly with its external aspect. And in such a history foreigners play the most important part. They have fought battles, conquered the country and ruled it. We have accepted this pressure from the outside, though at times efforts were made to shake it off and have met with occasional success. But on the whole this aspect of India's history reveals to our eyes, in its successive chapters, the failures of her people.

But it will have to be admitted that the Indian *sādhanā* does not identify itself with politics. True it is that great kings and emperors arose in our country; but their greatness has been quite their own. This sort of greatness owes nothing to the people who neither create it or participate in it with any pleasure. It developed along with one's individual power and dwindled with the same.

But India has a *sādhanā* of her own and it belongs to her innermost heart. Throughout all her political vicissitudes its stream has flowed on. A wonderful feature of this has been that it does not glide along any embankment of scriptural sanctions, and the influence of scholasticism on it, if any, is very small. In fact, this *sādhanā* has mostly been unscriptural and not controlled by social laws of any kind. Its spring is within the innermost heart of the people whence it has gushed forth in its spontaneity and broken through the barriers of rules, prescriptive as well as proscriptive.

Most of the persons from whose heart this spring has come forth belong to the masses and whatever they have realised and expressed was 'not by means of intellect or much learning of the sacred lore' (*na medhayā na bahunā śrutena*).

If we could visualise the historical development of this *sādhanā* we should discover where the living history of India exists. Then we might know after what ideal India has moved on from one period of her history to another, and how far she has realised that ideal. The long course, which the stream of India's cherished ideal has followed through the ages, has been traced in these lectures in all its major and minor branches by my esteemed colleague and friend, Professor Kshitimohan

Sen. We have seen how deeply true is this stream and how essentially it is India's own. The natural genius for *sādhanā* which is latent in the Indian people has been discovered in these lectures by Prof. Sen. The line of development, which its expression has taken amidst different internal and external obstacles, has been sketched in this work. We still expect to see at some future date a detailed history of its progressive movement. Unless we have this history, the true picture of India will remain only partially known to her children and such a partial knowledge might be very erroneous.

Santiniketan,
27th December, 1929.

RABINDRANATH TAGORE

# PREFACE

That there may come at any time an invitation from any learned society for delivering a lecture on the history of spiritual quests of the Mediaeval India never occurred to me before. It is nearly thirty-five years ago that in my young days I came to know in Benares *sādhus* and *santas* of various sects. It was a matter of happy accident that I was born in Benares which was a favourite haunt of them all. Possibly due to this fact I could get some opportunities in this field. So charmingly deep and liberal were the *sādhanā* and the sayings of those old *sādhus*, that I felt an intoxicating attraction for them all even at a very tender age. During my student life too I passed most of my time in studying these sayings. Luckily enough I secured then the favour of some good guides in this field, the like of whom it is very hard to meet now-a-days. Persons of this type are growing less in number every day. It was only the other day that Bābā Mohan-dās the old *sādhu* of Lakhan-kā village in Bhawnagar (Kāṭhiāwāṛ) passed away in Santa Cruz, Bombay. He had more than three thousand *bhajans* in his memory. In the first part of the selection from the sayings of Kabīr edited by me I have referred to some such *sādhus*. Many, however, were the able *sādhakas* who left this world without attaining any celebrity among scholars.

There are collections of many sayings of *sādhakas* stored up in manuscripts preserved by members of different sects and their *maṭhs* in different parts of India. In many of the *maṭhs* the custodians of these treasures preserve them with the zeal of the *yakṣa* of the Indian folk-lore and no one can see them even at the cost of his life. The same is the condition in the libraries of many ruling chiefs of Rajputana. It is not without a bitter experience that one is inclined to make a complaint of this kind against these institutions.

*Sādhakas* of the Indian Mediaeval age were mostly from the lower strata of the society, but sects which their teachings gave rise to, have tried afterwards in various ways to pass them as men of the higher castes. Thus many sayings of such *sādhakas* had either to be left out or distorted.

An enquiry into the family history of

Kabīr and Dādū will make this process very clear. The fact that Kabīr was the son of a Mahomedan weaver has been sought to be obliterated by many absurd stories. But historical criticism has mercilessly exposed such frauds. It cannot now be doubted that Kabīr was born in a Jolā family. And as for his initiation it was not at all a singular affair, for Rāmānanda had many such disciples: and moreover many *sādhakas*, even after Rāmānanda departed from this life, were influenced by his doctrines and hence declared themselves to be disciples of the master. We have referred to these things in the body of this work. Some among the followers of Dādū try to smother the truth about his birth by saying that he was the son of a Nāgar Brāhman. There are however some who say that Dādū, being the *Nirañjan* (God) himself, had no birth in the wordly sense. But truth cannot be suppressed. The late Pandit Sudhākar Dvivedī was of opinion that Dādū was born in a family of leather-workers who manufactured *moṭe* or leathern water-bags for drawing water from wells. This however is a partial truth. It has now been discovered that Dādū was born in the family of cotton-carders. The sources of our information have been the

*Jīvanparchayi* by Jan-gopāl, the *Pantha-prakhyā* by Dāsjī and the writings of Tejā-nand. In the absence of support from any other scholar I would have hesitated to make any statement on this point. But Rai Saheb Chandrikā Prasād Tripāṭhī who has equal regard for Dādū's doctrine and historical truth, has very clearly written about this. The keepers of those *maṭhs*, which furnished him with documents in the shape of old manus-cripts, have now begun to burn in their anger those old and rare works.

Authentic information in this line can however be had from those *sādhus* who have turned to the spiritual life due to an inherent love for it and have not allowed themselves to be held by the bondage of sects.

The sectarian *sādhus* do not care to recog-nize these deeply spiritual souls who are out-side any sect. But any one who is willing to have really genuine and old things and say-ings full of deep meaning, will have to seek their help.

It should be mentioned here that in the sectarian collections we very often miss the really deep and liberal sayings of Mediaeval *sādhakas*, which are available only from the *sādhus* who do not belong to any sect.

With the change of time and circumstances the number of such *sādhus* is gradually growing less and less. They are not like the modern *sādhus* who but for some noble exceptions are as good as professionals, or propagandists. Hence in spite of various kinds of 'Sannyāsis' that the modern spirit is calling into existence, the successions of the old-type *sādhus* are daily coming to an end. It may happen that after a time they will exist only in people's memory and even that much may not remain; for people in general are so very ignorant of them.

But, for writing a true history of the religious and spiritual efforts of Mediaeval India we have no materials other than those which have been enshrined in the sayings and doctrines the *sādhus* of the period and historical anecdotes about them.

The most important thing about India has been her religious and spiritual life. That she has made an effort to bring about a synthesis in the midst of diversities of various kinds has been the most prominent aspect of her history. From period to period this effort has been continued through successive generations of her great *sāhdakas*, and has concerned itself with her one problem. Political activities have never occupied a very important position in Indian history. Hence to understand the secret Soul of India we cannot do without collecting and studying the sayings and doctrines of various *sādhus* that have been preserved by their followers or the keepers of many sectarian *maṭhs*.

Had this been the situation in any progressive country of the West we might have seen that a number of young men would undergo great hardship in order to have access to these sources, and various institutions of the land would be reverently furthering researches in this line. But to expect similar activities in the present condition of our country would be hoping against hope.

From my coming to Santiniketan in 1908 I have been continually spending my holidays, vacations and other leisure hours in the study and investigation of the materials mentioned above. For a long time I kept everything to myself. But afterwards Rabindranath Tagore chanced to know of my activities and urged me again and again to publish the result of my studies.

But I felt a shyness over the proposal and thought that no publisher would be forthcoming to undertake the risk of publishing what to the best of my knowledge had yet no market. Authorities of the Indian Press, Allahabad however came forward to undertake publication, and as a result of the Poet's pressure I had to publish four small volumes, which included only a selection from the most important of Kabīr's sayings, while for an adequate representation of this *sādhaka's* greatness no less than ten such volumes were necessary. We have come to know as many as two hundred such *sādhakas* of Mediaeval India, whose sayings, it may be hoped, will render assistance to humanity in its march to spiritual as well as moral and social progress. This field is indeed vast, but the workers are few and those who have a genuine interest in such things are fewer still.

During my studies and investigation of the subject I have received great encouragement and assistance from Tagore. At the outset of this Preface I have mentioned that, it never occurred to me that these studies would ever find favour in learned circles. I began work by utilising my leisure hours only. But Tagore very generously gave recognition to the subject in his Visvabharati and thus enabled me to devote my whole time to it. I am sorry to say that young men who are to build up our future are still almost absent from the field. The little interest which some of them evince in this line can at best be called a condescension to the subject for the sake of writing out a thesis meant for some higher degree. But we can scarcely hope to obtain a high quality of work from such people.

The late Sir Ashutosh Mookerji who as a great scholar and educator, had for his life's supreme mission the building up of a true University once expressed a desire to have a long talk with me on this subject. And I did actually meet him and he discussed in various ways whether any scheme for the furtherance of such studies could be made. He had in his mind plans for doing many things but his very sad and untimely death put a stop to everything.

The invitation which came to me last year from the University of Calcutta to deliver the *Adhar Mookerjee Lectures* for the year 1929 was a surprise for me. I never expected, as I have said before, that any learned society would pay attention to the ideas and ideals of those illiterate *sādhakas*. I do not know who was instrumental in causing such a thing to happen. Hence my cordial thanks go to the entire executive authority of the University of Calcutta. My subject is vast and it is difficult to do justice to it in a lecture or two. But we may hope that before our own power of work will gradually become less and less the young promising students of our country will gradually take the responsibility of this work upon their own shoulders.

Those who assume this responsibility will not go unrewarded. Any one taking to this line will see that there cannot be any experiment in the field of religious and spiritual endeavours that has not been carried out by one or other of the *sādhakas* of the Mediaeval India. Being quite innocent of any scriptural knowledge these *sādhakas* never trod on the beaten track; and their genius and vision were ever free. Sects conforming to some kind of scriptures or other blindly followed the tradition while each one of these *sādhakas* used his vision to find out a new way of his own. Following these ways we shall meet with instances of boldness which have been evinced in handling the good and the evil in the human mind. Attempts from various sides to satisfy the spiritual hankering will also be seen. It is a pity that such a plenty of materials for discussing human culture has been lying unexplored. We remember in this connexion the Bengali *bhakta* Rām-prasād who said:

"O mind, you do not know agriculture. Without any cultivation lies this field of human existence which properly tilled might have led to the production of a golden harvest."

We who are fettered by our tradition and obcessed by our written literature do not care to see what vast wealth is passing away before our very eyes. Even now, if we make great efforts we may be able to save a small portion of it. Our information would cover barely one-sixteenth of whatever once existed. The remaining portion has already perished and the extant portion will possibly vanish rapidly. One studying them will see how the sayings of these unlettered *sādhakas* are often more deep and sublime than written scriptures. The authors are mostly illiterate and their *sādhanā* includes developing love among the different schools of *sādhanā* and synthesis of them all. This synthesis in spite of all its external difficulties is the true ideal of Indian *sādhanā*.

The opportunity which I have been allowed has been utilised in barely giving a glimpse of that *sādhanā*. It has been merely an outline. It is my desire that on some future occasion I shall try to give a fuller history of the age in which such a *sādhanā* prevailed. By a mere skeleton of it we cannot give any adequate idea. Without blood and flesh upon it, its living forms become difficult to comprehend. Some account of the achievements of the *sādhakas* and their sayings are needed for visualizing a correct picture of that age.

Many workers are needed for this vast field of researches, and hence I invite the young scholars of our country to this work. My heartful thanks go to the authorities of the University who gave me this opportunity of saying these few words and I am also to remember here again the great educator, late Sir Ashutosh Mookerjee.

My thanks are also to my young friend Mr Manomohan Ghosh who very kindly helped me in the correction of proofs and other matters. To all others who were of help to me in one way or other I express my gratefulness.

Last but not the least I am to acknowledge my deep debt of gratitude to Rabindranath Tagore who possesses a great reverence for the *sādhakas* of Mediaeval India as well as a rare power of appreciation and enjoyment of their deep and sublime sayings. The enthusiasm and reverence which Tagore cherishes for them have been of great help to me while working on these sayings. I am glad that his blessings in the shape of a Foreword from his pen have adorned these pages.

Santiniketan,
14th January, 1930.

KSHITIMOHAN SEN

# PREFACE TO THE TRANSLATION

In March 1929 I delivered *The Adhar Mookerji Lectures* in the Calcutta University. In the limited space of those Lectures I had to review the broad outlines of the history of the spiritual quest of medieval India, to which full justice could only be done in a more elaborately treated work. However, as I have studied facts from a new angle of vision, even this short sketch may have some value for the student of Indian thought and culture. This is my excuse for placing before public the English version of these Lectures, delivered originally in Bengali.

The English title of this work, Medieval Mysticism of India, will probably require some explanation, for the word 'medieval' naturally calls up to our mind a host of ideas associated with the European Middle Ages and one may well surmise some similarity between the Christian mysticism of those ages and the mysticism of Medieval India. But nothing can be further from the fact.

The chief characteristic of the typical Indian mystics was that they did not submit to the control of any church (i.e. sectarian organization) or scriptures (*śāstras*). This freedom in the matter of spiritual culture which was well-nigh non-existent in medieval Europe gave Indian mystic experiences a richness and variety which we shall look for in vain elsewhere.

Rich though it was from its early (Upanisadic) period, Indian mysticism became doubly so when Islam came to be a power in India. Impact of this new and powerful faith released the latent forces of India's religious life, and it was by her mystics that a synthesis was sought to be brought about between the conflicting elements of the two. Those who achieved and guided this synthesis were persons who, due to their birth in the so-called lower classes of society, were free from the bondage of scriptures or of any institutional religion. Another very important fact about them was that they had no ascetic aversion to life and its responsibilities and, in this respect too, they stand in sharp contrast to the Christian mystics of Europe. These facts explain the vigorous and marvellous development of mysticism in medieval India.

My thanks are due to the Calcutta University for giving me permission to publish these Lectures in an English translation. And for actually translating them I am to thank very warmly my young friend Mr. Manomohan Ghosh who made every effort to make this translation a readable one. To my esteemed friend Mr. C. F. Andrews too I am to express my sincere thanks for having very kindly gone through the entire translation in manuscript.

One aspect of the translation should be mentioned here. A number of Indian terms which, I think, have no exact English equivalents, have been given in transliteration and these have been defined in alphabetical order in the beginning of the book. As regards the transliteration of Indian words I have to some extent deviated from the accepted standard. This modification has been made for the convenience of the general reader.

In the Appendices I have reprinted four of my own articles published in the Visvabharati Quarterly. They, it is hoped, will to some extent supplement the reader's knowledge of India's Medieval mysticism presented in the Lectures in broad outlines.

KSHITIMOHAN SEN

Santiniketan,
20th December 1935.

# CONTENTS

APPENDIX II



APPENDIX III



APPENDIX IV

## CORRECTIONS

| | | | | | |
|---|---|---|---|---|---|
| Page | 12 | line | 8 | *read* | Qutabuddin *for* Kutabuddin |
| ,, | 19 | ,, | 2 | ,, | Jahangir *for* Jehangir |
| ,, | 20 | ,, | 14 | ,, | Bihar *for* Behar |
| | | ,, | 28 | ,, | basharā' *for* basharāh |
| ,, | 26 | ,, | 24 | ,, | the princess Jahānārā |
| ,, | 28 | ,, | 2 | ,, | that of Karim *for* that Karim |
| ,, | 71 | ,, | 23 | ,, | from any one. |
| ,, | 76 | ,, | 15 | ,, | Anantānand *for* Anantādand |
| ,, | 85 | ,, | 18 | ,, | Sāhib *for* Shāhib |
| ,, | 125 | ,, | 24 | ,, | disciple's *for* discipl's |
| ,, | 134 | ,, | 19 | ,, | Chhapra *for* Chapra |

# INDIAN TERMS

*abhaṅg* A kind of metre used by saints of the Mahārāṣṭra. The term is also used for a stanza composed in this metre.

*ajapā* The muttering of God's name with every breath —the kind of muttering which needs no rosary for taking the count.

*aṅga Lit.* 'limb'. Chapter of an anthology of saintly utterances.

*ārati* Waving a cluster of lights before the image of deity as a part of the evening worship. A song composed for this occasion.

*āsan* Skt. *āsana*. A posture helpful in the practice of meditation (see. Patañjali's *Yoga-sūtras,* II. 46).

*ātman* Self. The Supreme Soul. The individual soul.

*avatār, avatāra* Skt. *avatāra Lit.* 'coming down.' The coming of God (Viṣṇu) among mortals in human or in some animal form. Every time he so comes he is called an *avatār* in that particular form.

*badnā* A water-pot with the spout of a kettle. It is used by Muhammadans.

*behāg* A musical mode, proper for the mid-night.

*bhajan Lit.* 'Service'. Hymn, or singing of hymns.

*bhakta* Devotee. One who has *bhakti* (defined below).

*bhakti* Devotion. *Bhakti* has been defined as the supreme attachment to the Divinity.

*bharukā* A water-vessel with a straight spout.

*Brahman Lit.* 'vastness'. The Infinite. The Supreme Soul. This term is often used without the definite article.

*Brāhman, Brāhmaṇ* A member of the Hindu priestly caste. Its anglicsed form 'Brahman' has been not been used for avoiding confusion with the *Brahman* defined above.

*chamār* Leather-worker.

*dargāh* Tomb.

*darwājā* Door, gate.

*deha-tattva* Mystical theory of physiology held by some devotees of Medieval India. Their idea is that the entire cosmos is in this human body and a man can attain fulfilment of his life's object if he can only know this inner cosmos.

*dewan* Minister.

*dhoti* Cloth worn to cover the body from waist below.

*dohā* Name of a metre used in Hindī, Rājasthānī etc. A stanza composed in this metre.

*fanā* A term used by the Sūfis, see p. 13.

*fatwa* A religious edict

*guru* Spiritual guide.

*gotra* A group of families or clans.

*homa* Offering oblations to gods by pouring clarified butter into the sacrificial fire. This is a Vedic institution.

*holī* Spring festival. A musical mode specially suited to such a festival.

*japa* Muttering.

*jñāna* Knowledge. Knowledge of the philosophical scriptures or philosophy.

*Jolā* A Muhammadan weaver.

*kamala-bedha* The six mysical circles (*ṣaṭchakra*) or lotuses are supposed to exist in the human body which a *sādhaka* has a pass through before he reaches the final goal and attains beatitude. The piercing or passing through these lotuses placed one above another is called the *kamala-bedha*.

*kathaka* A narrator of Hindu mythical stories with a devotional content.

*kathakatā* The art of a kathaka who in course of narrating mythical stories uses recitation, songs and suitable gestures.

*kaupin* Loin-cloth.

*kāzi* Civil judge (among Mussulmans).

*kirtan* Singing the praise of God in chorus and often in accompaniment of cymbals and some kind of earthen drums (*mādals*). This is an institution associated mainly with the Bengali Vaiṣṇavas.

*kripān* A sword. Such weapon as the Sikhs are bound religiously to keep with them always.

*kuṇḍaliā* A metre of Hindī.

*mahanta, mahānta* An overseer of a shrine or *maṭh*.

*mantra* A Vedic hymn or prayer. A formula (of prayer) sacred to any deity.

*maṭh* Skt. *maṭha* means a boarding of celibate scholars. The word *maṭh* has thus come to mean an abode of celibate novices of any religious sect or headquarters of any religious sect where the guru and his associates live.

*mazār* A ṭomb. A grave.

*mallār* A musical mode suitable to the rainy season.

*muchi* A leather worker, shoe-maker, cobbler.

*moṭe* A large bag made of cow or buffalo hide for drawing water from wells for the purpose of irrigation.

*nauvat-khānā* A elevated place often above the main entrance to a house or town, where music is played with the beat of kettle-drums at regular intervals every day.

*namāz* A prayer to God by Mahomedans.

*pad* Skt. *pada* one-fourth part of a couplet. But it means also a couplet, poem or song as well.

*panth* *Lit.* 'way' Sect. e.g. Kabīr-panth, 'the sect of Kabīr.'

*panthī* One who has been in a Sect. e.g. Kabīr-panthī, 'one who is in the sect of Kabīr.'

*Para-brahma* The Supreme Soul. Almost the same thing as the *Brahman* defined above. Th adjective '*para*' simply intensifies the meaning. Parabrahma thus becomes the Highest Entity.

*paygambar* He who has come with a message of God *i.e.* a prophet (in Islamic theology).

*prema* Love. Attachment and regard existing between husband and wife. Love for God and all creation.

*puruṣa* Man. Personal God. The soul (as in the *Sāṃkhya-darśana*).

*rāg* Skt. *rāga*. A musical mode consisting of particular sequence of notes. There are six principal *rāgs*, and to each of these are attached six *rāginīs* which have some sort of affinity.

*ras* Skt. *rasa*. *Lit.* Sap, juice; taste, flavour, relish, pleasure. It thus has come to mean also the delight arising out of communion with God.

*rauzā* A mousoleum.

*rekhitā* A metre of Hindī.

*riṣi* A seer. One who has composed some hymn or hymns of the Veda.

*śabda* or *sabad* '*Lit*. word. It means particularly songs of a religious teacher. Cf. *vāṇī*.

*sādhaka* This Skt. word is derived from the root *sādh* meaning 'to accomplish, to conquer'. Hence the word means one who is accomplishing or is striving for accomplishment of his spiritual ideal and which striving involves the conquest of his senses and other disturbing factors. In the narrow sense the word is also used to indicate one who is out for acquiring some occult powers.

*sādhanā* The career of a *sādhaka* (defined above).

*sādhu* It is almost a synonym for *sādhaka* (defined above) but it has come also to mean any one who lives a pious life.

*sahaj* or *sahaja Skt. sahaja Lit.* Natural, simple. A non-ascetic teaching which recognizes and admits the natural demands of our life.

*saṃkīrtan* Singing the praise of God, in chorus, (sometimes) by people going in a procession in the public street; see *kīrtan* defined above.

*sannyāsī* A mendicant. One who has renounced the world.

*śāstra* Ancient Hindu writings on the social and other duties of man. It has two main sections; Vedas and Smritis.

*ṣaṭchakra* see *kamalabedha*.

*satsai* A collection of 700 stanzas.

*svāmī* Master. This term is used honorifically before the name of asceties or religious men of high order.

*sizdā* Prayer in a position in which one stoops so as to touch the ground with one's forehead.

*subedar* Owner of an administrative division of a province. (*subā*).

*śāl-grām* Skt. *śālagrāma*. A kind of stone considered to be the symbol of Viṣṇu and hence held very sacred.

*śākta* One who worships Śakti. the consort of a deity who symbolises his power. Worshipper of a goddess.

*śakti* See *Śākta* (defined above).

*śloka* A stanza of 32 syllables.

*sparśamaṇi* Philosophers' stone.

*śrāddha* A ceremony performed in honour of the departed man by his relations.

*śūnyatattva* The principle or the doctrine of the Void or Non-existence. (See Kshitimohan Sen. 'The Conception and Development of Śūnvavāda in Medieval India' in *The Visvabharati Quarterly*, New Series, Vol. I, Pt. I).

*tilaka* A mark or marks on the body (especially in the forehead) with yellow clay, sandal paste etc. This mark sometimes indicates the sect of a man.

*tulsi* Skt. *tulasi*. Sacred Basil plant.

*vāṇi* Message, sayings of a saint, mostly versified.

*vasanta* Spring, a metre and musical mode specially suited to spring.

*vrata* A religious act of devotion or austerity, vowed observance.

*yātrā* A kind of popular dramatic opera which is performed generally during the religious festivals held in honour of Viṣṇu-Krisna.

*yoga* *Lit*. joining, union. In connexion with religious and spiritual matters it means an union of the individual soul with the Supreme Soul by meditation, concentration of the mind and contemplation of the Supreme Spirit.

*yogī* One who strives for *yoga* (defined above).

*zamindar* A land-owner who has tenants.

## TRANSLITERATIONS

Sounds in Sanskrit except those mentioned below have been transcribed according to the system adopted by the J. R. A. S,

*ri* represents ऋ as well as रि or - *ri*
*ch* ,, च
*chh* ,, छ
*ṛ* ,, ड़ *i.e.* cerebral *r*
*ṛh* ,, ढ़ *i.e.* cerebral *rh*

The final *a* of Sanskrit, which is often lost in the vernacular pronunciation has been omitted in the transliteration. Both the Skt. and the vernacular forms of some words will, however, be met with in this work.

# MEDIEVAL MYSTICISM OF INDIA

তুমিই সাগর আমিই তরী তুমি খেওয়ার মাঝি,
কূল না দিয়া ডুবাও যদি তাতেই আমি রাজি,
( ওগো ) তোমা হৈতে কূল কি বড় ভরম কি আমার ?

—গঙ্গারাম

I am the boat, and Thou art the sea, and also the
boatman.
If Thou dost not take me ashore, but let me sink,
I grudge not; why should I be foolish and afraid ?
Is the reaching of the shore a greater prize than
losing myself in Thee ?

—Gaṅgārām

## LECTURE I

# ORTHODOX THINKERS

When the Aryans came down to India, the land was already enjoying a wealth of different cultures, Dravidian and pre-Dravidian. These cultures had their own paraphernalia—rituals, laws and customs etc.—and were not wanting in anything of this kind. But the Aryans too brought along with them their own rituals, laws and customs. The result was, that the Aryan and the pre-Aryan civilisations acted and reacted upon each other for centuries, and ultimately began to coalesce into one great Indian culture.

But this newer creation was possible, because forces which combined to produce it were themselves still living, that is, endowed with the vital principle of assimilation.

The influx of many new tribes from outside her borders did not yet cease while India's civilisation was still in the making. Names of many such tribes are to be met with in the pages of the Rāmāyaṇa, the

Mahābhārata and the Purāṇas. Scythians, Huns and such other tribes gradually became merged into the great social organism of India, because at the time of their coming the society of this country was not yet devoid of life which is to be characterised by its power of assimilation. These foreign tribes though they brought alien cultures were remarkably free from any rigid dogma or fixed creed which might be antagonistic to the Indian spirit; and besides this, till then India was able to receive new ideas and to assimilate them. It is for these reasons that, within a generation or two, those newcomers were filled with the religious spirit of India, and her ideas and ideals became quite their own.

That the Vedic ritualism gradually tended towards the Philosophy of the Upaniṣads and thinkers of the time were turning little by little into profound mystics, might have been due to a similar interaction of ideas and cultures. Things which were mere ideas in the Upaniṣads began gradually to give shape to human life and its spiritual longings. Mahāvīra, Gotama (the Buddha) and others gave impetus to this new current of idealism. At that time life and its inherent energy with its varied manifestation were still having their full play in different departments of Indian civilisation. In other words, Indians were still then a living people in every aspect of their life: in their religious principle and its practice, in the organisation of their religious sects or of society in general, management of kingdoms and empires, in arts and literature and in everything else. But later on, the people of the land began gradually to lose this mervellous power. Their religious life, social organisation, politics as well as common ideas, ideals and activities all came to be smaller and more narrowed by and by. This occurred at the beginning of the Indian Middle age.

This age however became again filled up with *prema* (love) and *bhakti* (devotion) when I s l a m's political power and its spiritual culture appeared in the land.[1] Observance of many complex rituals and various superstitious practices as well as an excess of emotionalism which were smothering India's natural devotion and love of God, received a rude shock from the political power of Islam, and this shock, together with its new kind of aggressive monotheism and staunch faith, brought awakening to the indigenous natural love and devotion and the monotheism that already existed in the land from a hoary antiquity. For in the Vedic *mantras* (hymns) where *ṛṣis* (seers) like Vasiṣṭha sang hymns in praise of Indra, Varuṇa and other deities we have *bhakti* in its incipient stage. But the Aryans on the one hand liked the formalism of sacrifice and other rituals, and on the other hand sometimes they evinced a leaning towards the pure knowledge of the *Brahman*. An abundance of the attitude of *bhakti* however existed among the Dravidians and probably other pre-Aryan settlers of the land. The intellectualism of the Aryans when it blended with the early cult of *bhakti* began gradually to make the religious spirit of India deeper and broader.

On the eve of the age of the Upaniṣads as we have seen before, an opposition to sacrifices and other rituals was gradually awakening deep mysticism in the heart of the Indian Aryans. This mystic element together with *bhakti* and *prema* began to influence the popular mind. Later on when the Buddhists broadcasted in India their purely intellectual *dharma*, this also had the effect of further deepening that influence. Gradually the Buddhists also received in their turn a profound influence of *prema* and *bhakti*.

Though it was due to a reaction of the worship of village deities, symbols and images, *bhakti* and *prema* increased in the heart of the people. Devotion of the Śaivas and Vaiṣṇavas is a proof of this. It must however be admitted that this *bhakti* at first was not of the ideal kind; the conception of the Divinity involved in it was very narrow indeed. But as the time passed it began to outgrow its original smallness. Though Śaivas and Vaiṣṇavas continued to utter the name of Śiva or Viṣṇu, the meaning of these words gradually came to be extended to the One and the Infinite, and thus every obstacle to the true *bhakti* vanished. The devotees developed the power of seeing through symbols.

Various weak points which developed in Indian society when Mahomedans first came to India, found expression also in a decadence of *bhakti* and of spiritual illumination. It has been mentioned before that these two things began to revive after the advent of Islam and its spiritual culture when Hindus in their attempt to meet the challange for superiority had to pay attention to the spiritual wealth of their forefathers which by that time fell into comparative disuse.

History has often proved that real strength does not lie either in the superiority of numbers or in the vastness of its extent. Thus millions of Hindus in spite of their marvellous heroism could not for a long time withstand the onslaught of a handful of foreigners. For, the latter though small in number were acting together under the inspiration of a living ideal, while the former by that time lost the binding force of any great idea which could inspire them for the defence of their own culture. But it must be said to the credit of India that she did not fall so quickly under the sway of the Mahomedans as did the Europeans. The unparalleled heroism which the fighters from different parts of India such as the Rajputs, Southerners and Easterners etc. showed in many a battle field stemmed the tide of invasion for some centuries. The Hindu society of that time began to be deficient in that living force by means of which it could absorb new-comers from outside the borders of India. And the Mahomedans, unlike the Scythians and the Huns brought along with them not merely different but contradictory ideas, ideals and creeds. For Islam had its exclusiveness of Semitic origin, which very carefully defined and maintained its boundaries. Even the inclusiveness that was natural in life came to be smothered in Islam by the pressure of artificial creeds and domgas. This latter fact made their assimilation in the Hindu society an extremely difficult affair. Temples, monasteries and other holy shrines gradually faced a great danger, and consequently the holier shrine of the heart which is the chief seat of the Spirit began gradually to flourish.

Lest India should sustain a defeat before the newly arrived ideal and its missionaries, the *sādhakas* of India began to rummage the treasure-house of the past to bring out those great ideals which fell into disuse and were forgotten; and they made efforts once more to hold them up before the public so that the latter might pursue them in their own lives. This was at the root of the spiritual activities of the Indian Mediæval times which found expression in the new *bhakti* and spiritual vision.

Just as the idols and holy shrines of the Dravidians, opposed though they were to the Aryan ways, awakened *bhakti* in the heart of the Vedic people, so the religious experience of the Mahomedans as well as their opposing ideals resulted in the awakening of the same *bhakti* in the Northern India. The great teacher R ā m ā n a n d a brought these two currents of *bhakti* together. .He gave up the use of Sanskrit, and in peoples' language preached about *jñāna* (knowledge) and *bhakti* to all irrespective of their castes. And Mahomedans also in their turn came to be influenced by this kind of idealism. A staunch faith, puritanism and pure monotheism which they brought along with them gradually began to be tinged with the colour of Indian thoughts. During her Middle ages India began afresh to replenish her treasure of ideas by a remarkable union of those two different kinds of idealism.

India, indeed lost her power but this power together with cause of its loss was external; her real strength still lay hidden within in a dormant condition, and for its full awakening it was waiting for the excuse of a chance below. This blow came at last with the i n v a s i o n o f t h e M a h o m e d a n s. It is for the reason of this great help of theirs in the spiritual awakening of Mediæval India that the religious history of this time should begin with a record of their spiritual efforts.

But one should not conclude that India of those days lacked a refined intellectualism or the power of penetrating thought. For, the great thinkers of the time were capable of astonishing the world by the subtlety of their marvellous power of analysis displayed with regard to logic and philosophy as well as art and literature. But sadly enough they gradually lost the power of creative synthesis and had before them no great ideal of life. Their ideal, vision and creative energy then came to be smaller, narrowed and weakened, and they paid all their attention to hair-splitting discussions.

The history of the period of the Mahomedan invasion is full of accounts of royal leaders and their allies. Time and again they have come down upon the land with host of their soldiery, and city after city and kingdom after kingdom fell before their victorious arms. But this surely was not the process by which one could attain success in the matter of conquering the heart of the people. Many of course became converts to Islam due either to greed and material advantages or to a threat of death and oppression administered by invaders and their militant followers, but the true conquest of India's heart could not be effected in this abominable way. It needed the coming of Mahomedan saints and *sādhakas* for accomplishing such a piece of work. And who but these people could satisfy them whose intense thirst for idealism made them look for a new truth and a new ideal? For, we need not repeat that conversion to Islam was never restricted to those people only who were guided in this matter merely by wordly interests or considerations, either by a greed of wealth and position, or by a fear of death and oppression, or by a feeling of revolt against the existing social or religious organisation. At a time when the socio-religious order came to be dissociated from a great truth, the blind and lifeless society failed to solve the problem of her neglected millions. Had these latter no other means of escape they would have become resigned to their fate and allowed themselves to be trampled on for ages. But a new force came to give them deliverance. *Sādhakas* came from abroad with their different ideals and began to settle in different parts of India. Under these circumstances those people, who were still an unsolved problem with the Hindu society, collected round these *sādhakas*. Places where the latter met their disciples and guided them to new truth gradually grew up to be places of pilgrimage.

But among these newly arrived personages too, those who were orthodox and intolerant Mussulmans could not win the heart of people so much, as did the *sādhakas* full of Sūfi idealism. Indeed there were many other factors that led to the numerical strengthening of Islam in India, but the root of its spiritual influence is to be looked for in the efforts of the latter class of idealists.

Due to natural reasons these illustrious new-comers appeared first in the Punjab and Sindh; for these places lay in the historic way by which foreigners came down to India. An account of these *sādhakas* must begin with the famous Makhdum Saiyad Ali al Hujwiri popularly known as Dātā-gañj Bakhsh or Al Jullāwi. He was an inhabitant of Jullāb and Hujwir near Ghazni. During his early life he travelled over many countries and finally made Lahore the field of his spiritual activities. It was here that his life came to a close. Even to these days many pilgrims—Mahomedans as well as Hindus—come to pay their homage to the saint at his tomb or *mazār* near the Bhāṭi Darwājā of Lahore.

From an inscription on its door we learn that he died in 1072 (465 A.H.).

Many pilgrims assemble around the tomb on every Thursday but the great annual fair takes place on the fourth Thursday in the month of Śrāvaṇa (August). The story goes that saints like Khwāja Muinuddin, Khwāja Kutabuddin Kāki, Khwāja or Bābā Fariduddin realised the highest truth after spiritual exercises on this very spot. Hujwiri's great work was the Kashf-al-Mahjub or the Mysteries Unveiled. It is a valuable help for the *sādhaka* of the Sūfi class. According to the local people he is the first preceptor of Sūfism in India.

A few years ago the present lecturer was a pilgrim to the shrine of Hujwiri and he saw that pilgrims had come there from different parts of the Punjab, such as the places of saints like Miān Mīr, Shāhdar Māli Shāh, Muhammad Goni, Pāk Donā Sāhib, Mādholāl Husain, Khwāja Sulaiman, and from *mazārs* of Mir Janjāni and Khwāja Sulaiman Tausi. The last two names belong to Lahore and Rawalpindi respectively.

In the Kashf-al Mahjub, Hujwiri has taught that, for at least three years the *sādhaka* should be under the care of a proper teacher. During the first year he should free himself from pride and serve the humanity. In the next he should harmonise all his actions with divine idealism and serve God. And in the third or the last year he will have to realise his own true nature, that is, to see through his own heart or 'within'.

With the Sūfis *fanā* is the term for a very deep mystic experience, and it means, paradoxically enough, dying alive or a total annihilation of the ego. According to Hujwiri, a vow of poverty with reference to spiritual efforts means a complete dissociation from every worldly object and an absolute abandonment of the ego with the intention of realising the All-embracing Unity. By this kind of realisation the *sādhaka* fully develops his eternal life; his animal nature enveloped in ego disappears and by the divine grace he overflows with a Godly idealism. Then his interest in things, as his own comes to an end; hence, an unnatural relationship (such as that of possession and exploitation) with them ceases altogether. This is *fanā*. He further says that one's individuality should be allowed to perish. A removal of all the worldly obstacles to spiritual efforts and a full attainment of real truth and a perfectly passionless condition constitute the state of *fanā*. A state of progress towards *fanā* is called *hāl* or *daśā* of the Bāüls and the Vaiṣṇavas respectively. Introspection, meditation, control of breath, uttering of *mantras* are its various means; but the success according to Hujwiri depends on the divine grace which is above all those means.

The influence of the Sūfis of the Chishtiyya school reached India next. Indeed Khwāja Ahmad Abdul Chishti (died in 966) the great founder of this school lived in the tenth century, but his doctrines were brought over to India by Khwāja Muinuddin Chishti who was born in Seistan in 1142. With a view to be in touch with all Sūfi teachers of the time he came *via* Khorasan to Bagdad. He met teachers like Karmānī, Kubrā, Suhrawardi and others. In 1193 he was in Delhi but as the place was not suitable for his spiritual activities he went to live in Pushkar a place of Hindu pilgrimage in Ajmer where he died in 1236. To the name of this saint Indian Sūfis accord an imperial honour. They call him Āftāb-i-

Hind or 'the Sun of India.' There assemble in his *dargāh* (tomb) a constant crowd of pilgrims, Mahomedans as well as Hindus. Akbar the Great is known to have travelled on foot to this place as a pilgrim. A special fair lasting for six days comes off here every year. A remarkable feature of this Sūfi shrine is that as in a Hindu temple, music is played here daily every three hours from the *nawbat-khānah* of *dargāh*, and around the shrine professional female singers of talents sing at the request of their rich pilgrim-patrons and earn enormous amounts in fees.

The spiritual activities of Muinuddin spread all over India, and even the Brāhmaṇs were not outside his influence. The present lecturer has seen in Pushkar, Ajmer, a class of people who call themselves Husaini Brāhmaṇs. They are neither orthodox Hindus nor orthodox Mahomedans. They have Hindu belief, customs and rituals together with Mahomedan ideas and practices. They say, "We are Brāhmaṇs, our scripture is the Atharva Veda in which the Hindu and the Mahomedan doctrines have been synthesised."

This admixture of rites and customs is the popular counterpart of the higher synthesis which united the *sāḍhakas* of those religions in a religion of love.

As we have said before they have Hindu as well as Mahomedan practices. In the matter of their choice of the latter they choose those only which do not clash with the Hindu customs. They have fasts in the month of Ramazan while Hindu days of fasts and *vratas* are also observed by them. Their women dress themselves like those of the Hindu. Those, whose husbands are living, wear special marks used by Hindu women of that category, and their male population utter the name of Husain while they go for alms. In their neighbourhood there are other sects of mixed Hindu-Mussulman type. But among them all, Husaini Brāhmaṇs are the most respected. In Rajputana and in the district of Agra Mālkānā Rajputs live like the Hindus. They utter the name of Rāma, observe Hindu practices and at times pay visit to *dargāhs*. In fact, they differ very little from the ordinary Hindus.

Priests or Kākās of the Imāmshāhi sect are something like the Husaini Brāhmaṇs. Members of the Shāhdullā sect also invoke the authority of the Atharva Veda and of Niṣkalaṅka (the Spotless

One) the great apostle of Hindu-Mahomedan synthesis. Khwāja Qutbuddin Kākī of Ferganah a chief disciple of Muinuddin after knocking at the door of many teachers, came at last to the latter and accepted him as the spiritual guide. He died in the same year as his guru. His tomb lies near Qutab Minar and many pilgrims assemble there even now.

Another chief disciple of Muinuddin was Shaikh Fariduddin Shakarganj. The sweetness which he realised in course of his meditation earned for him the title Shakarganj (Sarkara-ganj or a depository of sugar).* According to the Mahomedans the town of Ajudhan on the Sutlej in the district of Montgomery (the Punjab) received the name Pākpattan or the 'holy city' on account of Shakaraganj's holy association with it. Once Kilhan completely defeated the Mahomedans there. From this Pākpattan have gone out two roads, one to Dehra Ismail Khan and another to Dehra Gazi Khan. At the time of the Muharram, pilgrims come there even from Afghanistan and the far off Central Asia. It was due to Fariduddin's influence

* His followers believe in the story that pleased with his sādhanā God created lumps of sugar (*shakkar*=Skt. *śarkarā*) under his seat.

2

that Islam spread in the Southern Punjab. He preached that the gate of heaven was a very narrow hole. It was perhaps with this idea that a hole has afterwards been made there in a wall, and given the name 'the Gate of Heaven'. Those credulous pilgrims who aspire after an easy entrance to heaven pass through this hole with great difficulty in a particular moment (supposed to be auspicious) during the night of the Muharram. In 1265 Fariduddin left this world. The famous poet Shaikh Sharfuddin was his direct lineal discendant and was known to the world under his pen-name Mazmul.

Ahmad Sabir the founder of the Sabir Chishti sect was also Shakarganj's disciple. He died near Rurki in 1291.

The chief disciple of Shakarganj was Nizāmuddin Auliā who was born in Badaun in 1238. In his twentieth year he was nominated by his guru as his successor. The famous poet Khasru and Amir Husain Dihlwī were his disciples. The well known historian Zia-uddin Baranī too was his disciple. Many Hindu and Mahomedan pilgrims go to Auliā's *dargāh*. The *dargāh* of his saintly disciple Chirāgh-Delhi also is well-known.

The *dargāh* of Shaikh Salim Chishti is in Fatehpur Sikri. Jehangir's birth is known to have followed his blessings on the former's imperial parent. He lived in a cave, but Akbar, afterwards, built a *dargāh* for him. In 1572 he left this world.

In Sindh and the Punjab Chishti doctrines were broadcasted by Khwāja Nūr Muhammad who died in 1791.

The pioneer of Suhrawardi sect in India was Bahāuddin Zākariā who was born in Multan, and died there in 1266. He received his initiation in Bagdad. Saiyad Jalāluddin Surkhposh came from Bokhara and put himself under Zākariā's discipleship. He lived during the latter part of his life in Uchh where he died in 1291. His grandson Makhdum-i-Jahaniā. (died in 1384) was a famous *sādhaka*. Barhanuddin Qutab-i-Alam, a grandson of the latter went to live in Gujarat. He died in 1453 and his tomb in Baṭawā is a holy shrine for pilgrims. The *dargāh* of his son Shāh Ālam is in Rasulabad near Ahmedabad. This place is noted also for its natural beauty.

The founder of the Kādirī branch of the same Chishti sect was Abdul al Kādir al Jīlī. He was a great scholar, writer and orator. Saiyad Muhammad who brought the Kādirī doctrine to India, was a descendant of this master. He died in Ucch in 1517. The famous *sādhaka* Miān Mīr who belonged to this sect was much loved and esteemed by Dārā Shikoh who in his Shafināt-i-Auliā treated Miān Mīr's life and work. In 1635 this great man died in Lahore. Mullā Shāh who later on preached in Kashmir was a disciple of his.

So far about the Western India. In Eastern India too teachers like Shāh Jalāl of Suhrawardi sect in Bengal and Makhdam Shāh in Behar extensively preached their doctrine. Shah Jalāl died in Sylhet, Bengal in 1244.

Sūfi teachers tried as far as practicable to avoid any clash with the Koranic doctrines. But in spite of this a charge has sometimes been lavelled against them that they did not keep strictly to the ways prescribed by the Koran. In reply to this charge Muhammad Fazl Allāh was obliged to write a work named the Al Tuhful al Mursal-il-al-Nabī in which he established that Sūfism was not antagonistic to the Koran. Fazl Allāh died in 1620. He showed that Sūfis conform to orthodox ways (i.e. are *ba-sharah*).

These facts notwithstanding gradually there came up in Indian Islam many doctrines, the extreme heterodoxy of which could hardly be offered any effective check.

It is believed by some orthodox Mahomedan historians that, needed as were the Sūfis to conquer the heart of Indian people, the orthodox preachers of Islam became afterwards equally necessary for checking the heterodoxy which was thought to have grown up out of the very Sūfi doctrines. When the rigidly orthodox religion of the first Islamic conquerors failed to attract people, Sūfis like Nizāmuddin Auliā preached a religion of love which touched the heart of all and has been universally accepted by the time of the emperor Akbar. But during the time of A u r a n g z e b, the great-grand-son of Akbar, free-thinking developed among the *sādhakas* to such an extent that the orthodox emperor and his advisers could no longer remain indifferent to it. S a r m ā d who made himself conspicuous by his extreme neglect of conventional ideas excited the wrath of the emperor who got him executed. *Rubaiyats* (quartrains) Sarmād left are very well-known to Sūfis.

The free-thinking of Indian Sūfis advanced

more than anywhere else in Sindh. The ancestors of Faizi and Abul Fazl, the two friends and ministers of Akbar, came from Arabia and settled in Sindh first. Some generations later they migrated to Nāgore in Jodhpur. It is for this reason that Mubārak the father of Faizi and Abul Fazl had the title Nāgorī. This Mubārak Nāgorī was a thorough scholar in the philosophy and literature of Greece as well as in Islamic theology.

Though the father as well as sons of the family were well-versed in the Koran and allied literature there were among them no great regard for the scriptural injunctions. Faizi the eldest son of Mubārak (born in 1547) to whom Akbar gave the title Kavīśvara (the lord of poets) translated for the emperor the Mahābhārata, the Rāmāyaṇa and some Vedāntic texts into Persian. Besides these he wrote a commentary of the Koran, which surely was not from an orthodox point of view. Faizi was a member of Akbar's monotheistic group of Tauhīd-i-Ilāhī and was a tutor to princes. Abul Fazl, the younger brother of Faizi (born in 1551), became in his fifteenth year proficient in all branches of learning. After finishing his education he spent the first ten years in teaching and assisted his elder brother in his translation of Sanskrit epics. But all these works did not give him any peace of mind. In his famous history of Akbar he writes, that he passed the day-time somehow in various scholastic discussions, but during the night an inner restlessness robbed him of his sleep. Often he lelft his bed and went across the fields to humble cottages of fakirs who were full of spiritual wealth and were content to live an unostentatious life in the outskirts of the metropolis. But there he received nothing which could salve his sore within. Sometimes he thought of going to the wise men of China and sometimes to the monks of Drus. A longing for discussion with Tibetan lamas as well as Spanish monks sometimes overtook him while on other occasions he wished he could learn from the fire-worshippers of Persia the mysteries of the Zend-Avestā. He had no longer any faith either in the orthodox religion or in rationalism. For their undisguised free-thinking Mubārak's family offended very much the doctors of Islamic theology. So, to avoid molestation from those zealots they had to escape secretly to Agra, where the emperor Akbar gave them an unassailable shelter. Badāyunī, the orthodox historian of Akbar's time, was, as can very easily be expected, not very kindly disposed to these two brothers. He opined that it was they who spoilt the emperor. But of the two, Abul Fazl who was a great help in Akbar's free monotheistic movement,, received the attention of this historian more. For, "Abul Fazl," says Badāyunī "began to burn the world with the fire of his blasphemous views." The charges of the historian were perhaps not groundless, for Abul Fazl's critical attitude must have influenced many of his associates; for instance, in the monotheistic group of Akbar there was one Āziz Kukā who became very disgusted with the contemporary religious ideas and practices after he had witnessed the bigotry and superstition of the Mussulmans of Mecca.

It is well-known that Akbar always had around him a number of scholars who were mostly liberal in their views. The two most famous among them have been mentioned before. The name next in importance is that of Abdul Rahim Khān Khānān (1553-1629). He, also a minister of Akbar, was well versed in Persian and Arabic as well as in Sanskrit and Hindī. Besides this Rahim was a Hindī poet of considerable worth and wrote an admirable poem named the Rahim Sat-saī. He was a great friend of Tulsī-dās and was a staunch admirer of the latter's Rāmāyaṇ. A further evidence of his love of the Hindī literature is probably the tradition which ascribes to him the preservation of the most of Sūr-dās's devotional songs on Kriṣṇa.

So much about the liberal influences of Akbar and his circle. But his son Jahangir and grandson Shah Jahan were indifferent towards religious and spiritual questions. The story goes that on account of such an indifference Shah Jahan was once humiliated by Bābā-i-Koh, a Mussulman saint from hills. A very deep interest in spiritual matters returned however some generations later to Akbar's line. For, the Prince Dārā Shikoh the eldest son of the emperor Shah Jahan was from his nature given to think very deeply indeed about religious matters. He had a catholic heart and a noble vision and was capable of viewing different religious tenets synthetically. It has been mentioned before that he wrote a biography of saints named Shafināt-i-Āuliā. This prince had always around him Hindī and Sanskrit poets and saintly followers of Kabīr and Dādū. The famous scholar-poet Jagannāth Miśra was among them and the saintly Bābā-lāl of the Punjab was also a frequent visitor to Dārā's court. In a work named Majmual-Bahrain, or the Meeting of the Two Seas, Dārā made a synthesis of the Hindu spiritual doctrine and the Sūfistic tenets. He himself translated some Upaniṣads and some philosophical texts in Persian and got the same kind of work done by others. These translated works were given the title Sirr-i-Akbar. He had many ambitious ideas about creating amity among the followers of different religious systems and above all a synthesis of the Hindu and the Mussulman cultures.. But it is a matter of extreme regret that his career was tragically cut off before he could see his plans carried into action. He left behind him, however, some followers who for some time maintained their interest in his line of work. One of them was the princes Jahān-āra, his sister, and the other the prince Azam Shāh, a son of Aurangzeb. The latter was a patron of Hindī poets. His recension of the Satsaī by the Vaiṣṇava poet Bihārī is admiringly looked upon as the best of its kind even at the present time. Besides this, the Vaiṣṇava poet Dev who wrote Rasvilās, Prem-chandrikā and other works was Azam Shāh's protégé. This prince's partiality for Vaiṣṇava poets has been commented on by orthodox Mussulman historians as a sad lapse on the part of Aurangzeb's son.

From an account of the Sūfis of Sindh we have digressed into the history of Akbar and his circle as well as his illustrious scion Dārāh Shikoh. Let us now resume that topic with an account of the four saintly friends, Shāh Kalandar, Faridganj, Jamāluddin and Shāh Shakar. Born in Ghazni about the thirteenth century they were much troubled at the narrowness and bigotry of the current religious practices; then they resoved to migrate to some other land across the sea. Relying on God they left behind all their worldly possessions, and at the end of their travel reached Sehwan in Sindh. The local patriarchs (*pīrs*) however tried to drive them away but they persisted in staying there. Some time after, however, one of them went to Faridganj and another to Multan. The contribution of these four friends to Indian Sūfism is not small.

The next important name in Sindh is that Karim Shāh. He lived at about the year 1600. From his biography written in a language which is a strange admixture of Persian and Sindhi we learn that a Vaiṣṇava saint living near Ahmedabad gave him guidance in his spiritual life. This saint taught Karim to mutter the mystic syllable *'Om'* which according to his biography became for Karim a revolving lamp hung within a dark chamber.

Shāh Ināyat's is the next worthy name is Sindh. This universally adored saint lived in a much troubled time. For, Kalhorā princes of Sindh were then seeking merit by making converts to Islam under the threat of the sword. As a result of this many people in order to save their ancestral faith secretly escaped to Cutchh and Kāṭhiāwār. In his saintly retreat Inyāyat gave shelter to many Hindu families and saved them from molestation. For he did not believe that God was the monopoly of any particular sect. But this attitude enraged those fanatical Mussulman princes of Sindh who got him beheaded and sent his head as a present to the emperor of Delhi. This noble martyr is remembered and honoured even now by all local people as Bin-Sir or the beheaded saint.*

Shāh Latif the grandson of saint Shāh Karim (born 1689) the greatest poet and singer of Sindh was a prince among all the Sūfi saints of Sindh. He was universally respected by all communities of Sindh. Even now his songs are largely sung by people. In Bhiṭ connected with his saintly career Hindus as well as Mussulmans meet every Thursday night for spiritual exercises. Sometimes they sing and sometimes they all remain absorbed in silent meditation. Among songs sung there are those of Kabīr, Dādū, Nānak, Mīrā-bāī and other saints. (A collection of these songs has been preserved there in old manuscripts). This non-sectarian spirit is very prominent in Sindh. It occurs very often that a Mussulman is a guru (spiritual guide) to a Hindu and a Hindu is a guru to a Mussulman. They have carried on their *sādhanā* not only with the same love but also with the same language.

* Names comparable to his are Salārghāzi of Bahar-rāich, Bin-Sir of Panipat and Bābāchuṛā of Baṭālā and Lakkhe etc.

The names of Bedil and Bekas (1859) will practically close the list of prominent saints in Sindh. The songs of these two mystic poets are sung even now by people, and their tomb is a place where persons afflicted with sorrow and bereavement obtain their relief. Bekas was known earlier as Muhammad Husain, and died very young at the age of twenty-two. But his short life notwithstanding, he left a deep impression on the spiritual life of Sindh. The poets Sachal, Rohal and Kutab, too were persons of the same order. Their songs were beautiful and deep in meaning. In their *dargāh* pilgrims of all sects and sex keep vigil and sing. Among songs sung there are those by other saints irrespective of their Hindu or Mahomedan birth.

After Sindh let us turn to other parts of Northern India in the quest of prominent spiritual people of Islam who illumined Muhammadan India by their liberal teaching.

It is not known who united Hindus and Mussulmans in Girot,— a place of pilgrimage in Shahpur in the Punjab. Mussulmans come here in the name of Jamali Sultan while Hindu pilgrims invoke Dayāl Bhāwan.

The *dargāh* of Bābā Fattu is in Kāṅgṛā Rānitāl. This Mahomedan devotee attained the summit of spiritual life through the grace of a Hindu saint Gulāb Sing, the Sodhi Guru.

In the district of Jhang is the place of the Hindu saint Bābā Sāhanā. His former name was Mihr. He got his enlightenment after the discipleship of a Mussulman saint and came to be known as Mihr Shāh. At his shrine in Jhang Hindus and Mahomedans unite in paying homage to his memory.[2]

There is a story that Shams-i-Tabriz by his occult powers brought under his control the heat of the sun as well as of fire. Both Hindus and Mahomedans visit this place of this saint who has been saddled with miracles.

The devotees of Musā Suhāg (15th century) dress as females and are comparable to the worshippers of Becharā Devī near Ahmedabad. Both these places are adjacent to each other.

Imām Shāh (15th century) of Gujarat founded a sect named Pīrāṇa panth or Kākā panth. It has eight branches but its original head-quarters are in Cutchh.

Followers of this sect are mostly Pāṭidārs. Though they have Hindu names and observe all Hindu customs except that their dead bodies are buried with Mussulman rites, they are disciples of a Mussulman guru. The Pāṭidār assistant to this guru is called Kākā (the uncle) who together with Brāhmaṇs are their priests. At the present time Kākā-panthis of Navsārī and neighbouring places are gradually turning to orthodox Hinduism. This sect has a Messiah named Niṣkalaṅka or Nakalaṅkī (the Spotless One) who is the tenth incarnation of Viṣṇu. They worship this Messiah. In these matters they are similar to the Pīrzāda sect of Bāhādurpur, Central Province. This sect was founded by Muhammad Shādullā in the middle of the seventeenth century. He culled edifying precepts from both the Hindu and Mahomedan scriptures and made these the basis of his synthetic religion. According to Shāhdullā too Niṣkalaṅka the tenth incarnation of Viṣṇu should be worshipped.

A similar confluence of Hindu and Mussulman *sādhanās* was a very frequent occurrence in later Mahomedan India. In the early part of the seventeenth century a Mussulman lady named Tāj wrote many devotional songs on Krisṇa. Besides this Saiyad Ibrāhim (*circa* 1614) who chanced to be under the spell of Vaiṣṇavism and its beautiful mystic songs, turned a Vaiṣṇava and himself composed similar songs which testified to the depth of his devotion. After his acceptance of Vaiṣṇavism, Ibrāhim came to be known as Ras-khān. Qādir Bakhsh, who was his disciple, too gave expression of his love for Krisṇa in beautiful poetry.

The Khojā sect which has many followers in Gujarat has been greatly influenced by Vaiṣṇavism. This was founded by one guru of Ismāiliā sect who began to initiate people like the gurus of the Vallabha school. Like the followers of Vallabhāchārya the Khojās are veritable slaves of their guru who to them is the incarnation of Krisṇa. They are merchants and exceedingly rich. Formerly they had Hindu names and customs, but are now turning gradually to orthodox Islam. But in Gaṛhṛā (Kāṭhiāwāṛ) some two hundred and fifty families have been absorbed by the Svāmī-Nārāyaṇī sect.

Among the Mahomedan literary men too there were persons of liberal views. Most of them, in their works, gave expression to what they thought about the amity of different religious sects and a synthesis of their tenets. Mālik Muhammad Jāyasī (1540) the disciple of the Chishtiyya *sādhaka* Mahiuddin was such a writer. He studied Sanskrit poetics (*alaṃkāra*) with Hindu pandits and wrote, under the inspiration of Kabīr's teaching, the Padumāvatī[3]—a beautiful Hindī poem treating allegorically the relation between the Divine Spirit and the individual human soul. The Hindu ruling chief of Ameṭhī was an admirer of Jāyasī. It was he who built the poet's *dargāh*. Gandharva-rāj, the chief pandit in the court of the Rājā Jagaddeva of Ameṭhī was an intimate friend of Jāyasī. The poet was childless, so he conferred his family name 'Mālik' on the sons of his friend from whom the present *Kathakas* of Rāipurā and Haldiā have descended. Jāyasī wished that his friend's descendants would all possess a sweet voice and use the same in the adoration of God. *Kathakas* of Rāipurā and Haldiā have still the word 'Mālik' added to their name.

Another Mahomedan poet in Jāyasī's line was Nūr-Muhammad (1744). Inspired by Jāyasī he wrote his poem named Indrāv a t ī. It is an allegorical poem like the Padumāvatī.

The liberal spirit and noble idealism which we have traced so long in different saints and literary men of Mahomedan birth did not become rare even up till very recently; for it is not a very distant event that H a s a n N i z ā m ī, the descendant of Nizāmuddin Auliā and *Hāfiz* of his *dargāh*, wrote a work with this rather lengthy title: *Hindustān-ke do paygambar Rām aur Krishna*: *Salāmu-Allāhi 'alaihim*. There he says, "According to the Koran, God sends his *paygambars* in all parts of the world. How can this be untrue with regard to India? So Rāma, Kriṣṇa and the Buddha are the *paygambars* of this country and the teachings of these seers carry authority."

We have already learnt that the religious Mussulmans coming from abroad were influenced by the Hindu *sādhanā*. But to understand the intensity of this influence we must attempt an account of the specific lines in which it worked.

If all Sūfi writers including Hujwiri have prescribed obedience to a guru this tenet was much extended due to a Hindu influence on it.

The Upaniṣadic cosmology, together with the words of Hājī Sabzwārī who said much later that the creation was a ray of the Divine Light, gave the Mahomedan *sādhakas* various newer theories of creation which bore unmistakable marks of their origin.

The mysticism of the Bātiniyās became mixed up with the spiritual philosophy of India and gave rise to many new schools which the orthodox doctors of Islamic theology branded as *be-sharā*' or heretical.

Some Mussulman *sādhakas* in the Punjab and elsewhere had a great fascination for the Yoga-system. In imitation of the Hindu works on the subject they wrote illustrated treatises dealing with *āsana*, *ṣaṭ-chakra*, *kamala-vedha* and the mysteries of the physical system. The present lecturer has seen in the Punjab several manuscripts of such works.

That the Āzād sect shaved themselves clean and denied the authority of the scriptures is most probably due to some sort of Hindu influence. Followers of this sect are often to be found in Jalaon.

The most remarkable among the Hindu influences on Islam is the acceptance of Tāntric teachings, by some Mahomedan *sādhakas*. Though the first available instance of this is the tenets of Rasūl Shāh of Alwar who belongs to the eighteenth century, such things surely began much earlier. To the followers of Rasūl Shāh who are well-acquainted with alchemy and poetical literature and are not averse to drinking, people ascribe many miraculous powers. Like the followers of the Tantra they sit in a circle (*chakra*) and observe Vīr-āchāra or 'the ways of the hero'. And they claim to be drinking, in the Tāntric fashion, the nectar of the *sahasrāra* (the thousand-petalled lotus) after piercing through the six circles (*ṣaṭchakra*) *via* īḍā, piṅgalā and suṣumnā.

An account of the Hindu influence on Islam will not be complete without noticing how the superstitious side of the two religious systems began to meet. Popular legendary heroes of the Mussulmans, like Ghāzī Miān, Pānch Pīr, Pīr Badar and Khwāja Khizr began to be worshipped as gods in the Hindu fashion. Another such new-fangled deity was Satya Pīr or Satya Nārāyaṇ of Bengal. This godling enjoyed the veneration of the Hindus and the Mahomedans alike.

Besides the above instances there are

cases where the Hindu influence on Islam, though not directly perceptible, must be postulated. For instance there are in Bengal two small groups of people named Bāül and Zikir who strictly speaking constitute neither a caste nor a religious sect. They call themselves neither Hindus nor Mahomedans though house-holders among them observe many Islamic customs. On account of this latter fact, preachers of the orthodox Islam made an attempt to reclaim them who appeared to have strayed from the fold, by publishing *fatwas* denouncing the Bāül doctrine. The present lecturer has seen some of these anti-Bāül *fatwas*. Both Bāüls and Zikirs are free from the Hindu as well as Mahomedan orthodoxy. Their spiritual exercises consist in songs and they are very liberal in their views which betray Vaiṣṇava as well as Sūfi influence.

Most of the teachers named hitherto have called themselves Mahomedans though the orthodox followers of the religion have not failed to denounce them as heretics. This latter section naturally raised protests in various quarters. Among such protestants the Farāizi sect of Eastern Bengal is worth mentioning. The founder of this sect

Hājī Shariatullā was born of weaver parents in a village of Faridpur. He made a pilgrimage to Mecca where he stayed for twenty years as a disciple of Shaikh Tāhir-al-Makkī. In 1802 he returned home and began preaching his views. He protested against an excessive obedience to guru on the part of a disciple, and said that India being under a non-Moslem power was *Dar-al-harb* or a country in war and was a place where 'Id and the *Jummā* prayer stood ceremonially barred. He exhorted every one to be strict followers of Islam and to give up worshipping *pīrs*, *dargāhs* and similar objects. Hājī Shariatullā's son Muhammad Muhsin *alias* Dudhu Miān organised his father's followers into different sections with a creed as follows:

"Within the Farāizī community there is no distinction between the rich and the poor; when an individual is in danger all the rest of the community are to come to his help."

"The earth belongs to God; hence no man has hereditary right to any land nor can he demand tax for its use."

Because of this creed of mutual help among them, members of the Farāizī community could offer successful resistance to a concerted action against them by *zamīndārs* and British Indigo-planters as well as other Mussulmans. Saiyad Ahmad of Western India too preached similar doctrine and helped to spread the Wahābi ideas.

Like the Mahomedans the Hindus too made efforts, in different ways, to keep their own religious and spiritual culture alive. A section of them tried to introduce liberal ideas with the maximum retention of old laws and customs, while the other section, in contrast with these virtual conservatives, in their attempt of creating an unity and synthesis paid least heed to old scriptures and customs. According to the Mahomedan theologians the first party is *ba-sharā'* or conformist, while the rival party is *be-sharā'* or heretical. Bāūls who have a very keen sense of humour characterise the reformers of the first school as 'fellows with a long tether' and the members of the other school as 'fellows with no tether'. This homely but apt simile is taken from the pasture where the animal tethered with a long rope can browse on a very extensive area but animals not tethered at all can practically have a bite anywhere. The latter's is the real freedom. In the Mediæval India conformist or 'long-tethered' reformers were called *Loka-*

*vedapanthī* or 'the followers of customs and scriptures' whereas the non-conformist or 'untethered' reformers were known as *Anabhau-sācha-panthī* or 'the followers of truth as experienced through intuition'. This first lecture is about the 'long-tethered' ones among the Mahomedans as well as the Hindus. The 'tetherless' ones of both the communities will form the principal subject of discussion in the second lecture. Up till now the Mussulman *ba-sharā'* or conformist group has been reviewed. Hence before concluding this lecture we shall attempt to give an account of the efforts of the conservative section of the Hindus for the preservation of their religious and spiritual culture. Facts connected with this attempt on the part of the Hindus are more or less known to you all; still to make our account complete the briefest outline of this history will be attempted here. A more elaborate treatment of the efforts of the Mahomedan *sādhakas* which has been made here, scarcely needs an apology; for, these worthy people may not be known to historians and the general public.

Before the Mahomedans came to India, Vedic customs and religion had already received the death-blow at the hands of heretics like the followers of Mahāvīra (Jina) and Gotama (the Buddha). But scholars like Sāyaṇa, Mādhava, Uvaṭa, Dūrga, Ānanda-tīrtha, Bhaṭṭa-bhāskara tried to give new life to this already decadent religion by their learned commentaries on the Vedas. Royal patronage to such works was however not wanting; for, without the interest taken in the matter by the king Bukka Harihara, Sāyaṇa could scarcely write his marvellous commentaries even in the fourtheenth century.

Next to commenting on the Vedas, the codification of laws was an important means at the hand of conservative reformers of Hinduism. But it was not very easy to enliven a decaying body by imparting fresh life into it; for, it has been mentioned before, that the much-decayed society was crumbling to pieces when the Mahomedans came to occupy India. At the time of such a rapid disintegration of the old social order, scholars like Medhātithi, Kulluka-bhaṭṭa, Vijñāneśvara, Hemādri, Raghunandana were making desperate efforts to save the society by furnishing clear laws in the shape of commentaries and digests containing passages from the ancient and rare law books which were once a great binding force among the Hindus. The vast amount of industry and erudition which these commentaries and compilers of digests have displayed is marvellous.

Philosophy too received attention of the defenders of the ancient religious culture of the land. Even from before the coming of the Mahomedans the famous Śaṅkarāchāryá and his guru tried to awaken all by means of knowledge. And at a time when the Buddhist monasteries were on the decline Śaṅkara established four monasteries for training monks who would preach his doctrines. This probably gave a new impetus to the study of the six schools of philosophy and a host of commmentators took up the field for enlightening the public on philosophical idealism. But the general mass of people were not much affected by these measures which were meant only for the learned.

A revival of the study of the Tantras—popularly but unjustly[4] believed to be mere source of corrupt practices became gradually an instrument in the hands of the conservative reformers of Hinduism. Valuable wisdom and deep philosophy contained in works like the Mahānirvāṇa, Kulārṇava and

Viśvasāra and other Tantras were first little known outside the circle of Vedāntists and professional scholars. Authors of these works wrote in a very simple style and made an admirable attempt to popularise the teaching of the Tantras.

In the Mahānirvāṇa Tantra an advocacy was made in favour of the realisation of the *Brahman* and the practices leading to it, to the exclusion of the worship of various deities. Meaningless social customs have been undermined, and to all persons irrespective of their sex and caste have been accorded the right to the highest form of spiritual self-culture. In brief, authors of such Tāntric texts tried to hold before the Hindus a new but perfect ideal of life. With this end in view, they, on the one hand, codified different branches of laws such as marriage, succession, contract etc. and on the other hand, they chalked outlines of spiritual advancement for the individual as well as for society. For the common people who did not care for larger social ideals and were satisfied with an ordinary religious life, Āgamavāgīśa Krisṇānanda and other adepts in the Tāntric lore prepared digests like the Tantrasāra giving guidance to different forms of worship. But, for those who were thirsty for deeper spiritual experience, Pūrṇānanda and other *sādhakas* described the *ṣaṭchakra* and gave exposition of the Yoga and allied subjects. And commentators who followed them attempted further elucidation of these things.

Followers of the Bhāgavata cult too contributed their share in the attempt made for the preservation of Hinduism. The popular belief among scholars regarding the origin of this cult is that it spread in this country along with the coming of tribes like Yadus, Turvasus, and Vrisṇis etc.; and this cult syncretising with indigenous religious ideas produced the unique cult of Bhakti. It received influence also from the Yoga doctrines. From the authors of the Pañcharātra literature, the Śāṇḍilya Sūtra and the Nārāyaṇīya chapters of the Mahābhārata down to Nārāyaṇa Parivrājaka and even some of his worthy followers of later times, attempts have been made to popularise the Bhāgavata cult. As this subject has been ably treated by scholars like Sir R. G. Bhandarkar* it will

* See his 'Vaiṣṇavism Saivism and Minor Religious Systems'.

be scarcely worth while to dilate on it in this lecture.

Just as the followers of Buddha made him the complete embodiment of all their ideals and aspirations, the worshippers of Śiva and Viṣṇu too tried to make these deities a symbol of all their ideals and aspirations. Their efforts continued down to the Mahomedan period of Indian history and gave strength to Hinduism.

The Āḷvārs of the Southern India created a strong following among numerous people mostly Vaiṣṇavas. To them utterances from the Divine mouth of the Āḷvārs (or the Tiru Vāymoḷi) in spite of their birth in untouchable families, were more honoured than the Vedas. Aṇḍāl, a woman was an Āḷvār; she and her father Viṣṇuchitta, an Āḷvār too, were from low caste, but they were greatly adored by people notwithstanding their very humble birth.

On love and devotion which are inherent in the human heart these Āḷvārs based their Neo-Bhakti cult. From the time of their successors like Nāthamuni, Āḷvaṇḍār-Yāmunāchārya, Pilley-Lokāchārya (the author of the Artha-pañchaka, 1213) this Neo-Bhakti movement progressed uniformly up to the time of

Rāmānuja; but afterwards it changed its form to some extent. Utterances of the *Bhakta* Āḷvārs created the sweet sap of devotion (*bhakti*) while later teachers like Nāthamuni and Yāmunāchārya tried to supplement the same by associating knowledge (*jñāna*) with it. In the caste-ridden Southern India of the twelfth century Rāmānuja preached devotion to Viṣṇu and gave a high status even to members of the lower castes. And he it was, who recognised the vernacular devotional works such as the Tiru Vāymoḷi of the Pariah like Thirupan Āḷvār as the Veda of the Vaiṣṇavas. But curiously enough he could not break the rules of caste. As followers of one religious doctrine, the worshippers of the Viṣṇu were equal, but caste rules divided them socially. To get over the difficulty a rule was, therefore, made that every one should take his meals separately. For the question of status among castes occurring only when different people are to dine together will not then occur at all. This makeshift method represents the Ten-kalai or the Southern school. Even in this school, Vedānta-deśika of the sixteenth century discovered some excessive freedom and re-introduced many old and Vedic customs among the followers of the Neo-Bhakti cult, and started what is called the Vaḍa-kalai or the Northern school.[5] Customs to which he gave a fresh lease of life included the performance of the Vedic *homa* in the marriage ceremony and the tonsure of women at the death of their husbands. These two customs were previously abolished by the Southern school.

Rāmānuja wrote the philosophy of the Neo-Bhakti cult. As the dualism preached by Rāmānuja was influenced by the monistic Vedānta it also goes by the name of the Qualified Monism (*Viśiṣṭādvaitavāda*). As plenty of good works on the subject are available it does not seem necessary to attempt here a summary of the same. Rāmānanda of whom we shall speak in our next lecture belonged at first to the sect of Rāmānuja but subsequently he seceded from it and became with his new ideas one of the great teachers of the Mediæval India.

Ānanda Tīrtha (1331) who was originally a Śaiva of Śaṅkara's school turned later on to Vaiṣṇavism and became the founder of *the Mādhva sect, which accepted dualism. In his spiritual method too Ānanda Tīrtha* shunned the Vedānta and inclined to the ways of the Sāṅkhya-Yoga.

In the beginning of the fifteenth century Viṣṇusvāmī preached Vaiṣṇavism, in the Southern India. As his doctrines were supposed to have come from Rudra (Śiva) his followers are said to belong to the Rudra sect. Lakṣmaṇa Bhaṭṭa—a descendant of Viṣṇusvāmī migrated to the Northern India where his son Vallabha preached 'Vallabhism' or the Way of Divine Grace (*Puṣṭi-mārga*). In his sect God is considered to be the embodiment of *satchidānanda* (Existence, Intelligence and Bliss). And the philosophy of this sect is known as Pure Non-dualism (*Śuddhādvaitavāda*). According to the followers of Nām-dev, Viṣṇusvâmī learnt *bhakti* from their master. Considering the chronological position of the two this does not seem to be improbable. Even in important sects like the Rāmānujis it is often found that great teachers have received inspiration from illiterate outcastes like some of the Āḷvārs.

Nimbārka's followers constitute another sect of the Vaiṣṇavas. They are known also as the sect of Sanaka or the followers of Monism-with-dualism. (*Dvaitādvaitavāda*). They hold the oldest doctrine. Chaitanya's doctrine is also called the Mādhvism of Bengal. For, an offshoot of the Mādhva teaching came to this province and gave new life to the Mahāprabhu or the Great Master (Chaitanya). Even before Chaitanya's time there were in Bengal Vaiṣṇava teachers like Iśvarapurī and Keśava-bhāratī, but it was the Great Master who preached the Neo-Bhakti cult of Bengal.[6] In his religious sect Chaitanya accepted different castes of Hindus as well as Mussulmans, but he failed to unite them socially. Caste-rules remained. Born in 1485 Chaitanya died in 1533. Before his time poets of early Vaiṣṇavism like Jayadeva, Vidyāpati and Chaṇḍīdās had influenced the people of Bengal. Thus after joining hands with Nityānanda, a powerful exponent of the Sahaja school the Great Master's teachings spread very easily. Later on, masterly writers like Rūp, Sanātan, Rāy Rāmānanda, Jīv Gosvāmī and Kriṣṇadās Kavirāj furnished the Master's doctrines with philosophical and theological foundation. During his life-time the Master's teachings were carried to Orissa and Vrindāvan. Later on, Assam too followed in the wake of Chaitanya, and Gossāins of the four shrines in Majuli (Assam) too preached his doctrines.

The Mahāpuruṣiyā sect of Śaṅkar-dev in Assam is a little more liberal than those Gossāins; for, he being a Kāyastha had to have less narrowness in social matters and made disciples of the aboriginal tribes (Nagas and Mikirs) as well as Mussulmans. One special feature of his teaching is that he strongly denounced worship of images and practices connected with it. Among his followers Śūdras too have, at times, Brāhman disciples.

Besides this, Vaiṣṇavas of Rajputana too were influenced by the school of Chaitanya. And the same influence of Bengali Vaiṣṇavism is perceptible among Bāniās of Balsār (Surat) as well as the inhabitants of the far off Dera Ismail Khan (Punjab). They all consider Vrindāvan and Navadvīp to be the most important among holy places and some of them sing some Bengali devotional songs.

People of the Vallabha sect are largely to be met with in Gujarat and Cutchh. We have already mentioned Vallabha's parentage. In 1479 he was born in Benares. His followers worship the deities Rādhā and Kriṣṇa with all possible pomp and show.

Vallabha's son Viṭṭhal was a Hindī prose writer of considerable worth. Four disciples of his father Vallabha, together with four of his own, were all poets exerting their literary powers on behalf of the cult of Krişṇa's adoration. These eight are collectively known as the Eight Stamps (*aṣṭa-chhāp*). The famous blind poet Sūr-dās was one of Vallabha's four disciples. According to one tradition six brothers of the poet fell fighting the Mahomedans, but the blind man could not fight and hence lived to become a poet of divine love. According to some authorities Sūr-dās's father was one of the musicians of Akbar's court and hence must have lived much later.

Another important name in the history of the Vallabha sect is Vrajavāsi-dās of Vrindāvan. The Vraj-vilās which he wrote in 1770 is a well-known work of the Vaiṣṇavas.

In course of time a manifold corruption set in among the followers of Vallabha. As a protest against this, Charan-dās in 1733 started in Delhi his new sect which has been called after him Charandāsī. His teachings are very much in agreement with that of Kabīr. Dārā Shikoh's works too gave him some inspiration. Another sect which arose in protest against the decadent Vallabha school was that known as Svāmī-Nārāyaṇī. Its founder Sahajānanda was born in 1780 in the village of Chhapaiyā or Chhippiyā in Goṇḍā (Oudh). Inspired mainly by seeing the devotion of a simple illiterate Chamār (leather-worker), Sahajānanda realised the urge of spiritual life and the essentials of religion in their simplicity and naturalness. This enlightenment impelled him to preach a pure religion. He fought against the Vallabhites and founded his Svāmī-Nārāyaṇī sect, the chief centres of which are in Baṛtal in Gujarat and Gaṛhṛā and Mūlī in Kāṭhiāwāṛ. This sect recognises the right of lower castes to a spiritual life and accepts Mahomedans too in its fold. It has been mentioned before that some 250 Khojā families have been admitted to this sect.

Members of the Rādhāvallabhī sect which arose from the Nimbārka or the Sanakādi sect consider, like the Tāntrics, *Śakti* to be superior to *Puruṣa.* Hence they put Rādhā before Kriṣṇa. In 1585 the *bhakta* Hita Harivaṃśa founded this sect in Vrindāvan. In Bengal too Vaiṣṇavism together with Tāntricism gave rise to different new doctrines. Vaisṇavas who are under the influence of the Tantras have more regard for Chaṇḍīdās, Nityānanda and Vīr-bhadra than Chaitanya, the Great Master. It may be that the Rādhāvallabhī sect was influenced by a sect which held similar views. There is nothing strange about this, for even Chaitanya himself had to carry on his mission in co-operation with people who held such doctrines. As for the similarity of the Rādhāvallabhīs with the Bengal Vaiṣṇavas it may be said that Nāgarī-dās of the former sect was looked upon by many as belonging to the latter group.

Under the influence of the Bengali Vaiṣṇavas the Haridāsī sect arose in Vrindāvan in the middle of the sixteenth century. Leading teachers like Viṭṭhal-vipula, Vihāriṇī-dās and Saha-charī-śaran (1763) were born within this sect. The poet Sītal Svāmī belonged to the Taṭṭī sub-sect of the Haridāsī sect and was born in 1723. There is a story that Mīrā-bāī who was traditionally known to be a disciple of Ravi-dās once met Jīv Gosvāmī of Vrindāvan. According to some authorities she was considerably influenced by the Vaiṣṇavism of Bengal. This point, however, is controversial. A critical examination of the same will be out of place in a general lecture of this kind. The name of the Marāṭhī saint Tukārām should be mentioned now. He gave up the scriptures (*śāstras*) and the sacred language (Sanskrit) and preached, in vernacular, his message of love and purity which reached the heart of people. Opinions differ as regards the time of his birth. Some say it occurred towards the end of the sixteenth century and some place the event in the beginning of the seventeenth century. Tukārām was a *Śūdra* by birth and was the son of a grain-merchant. He was a worshipper of *Viṭhovā* of Paṇḍharpur. Some people believe that Tukārām had intercourse with Vaiṣṇavas of the Bengal school, for his guru was Keśav-chaitanya or Bābājī Chaitanya.[7] Tukārām's *abhangs* which are very popular among the *bhaktas* of his province betray an influence of Nām-dev and other saints of the Mahārāṣṭra.

The centre of Nām-dev's sect is in Paṇḍharpur. He belonged to the tailoring profession and is usually considered to have preached between 1400 and 1430. His teachings travelled from the Mahārāṣṭra to the Punjab. The present lecturer has seen a *maṭh* of his followers in the village of Ghomān in Baṭālā (Punjab). According to the tradition available in this *maṭh*, Nām-dev was born in 1363 in the village of Narsi-Bāhmani in Satara, Bombay, and his guru was the famous Jñānesvar. Nām-dev was a householder and a married man. In his fiftieth year he renounced the world and travelled all over India and made acquaintances of saints and holy men. For sometime he stayed in Hardwār, but left the place afterwards for Ghomān in the Punjab, where he passed his last days. He met Phiroj Shāh (1355-1388) of the Tuglak dynasty. Shāh Ālam (1446) the last Saiyad King of Delhi granted some amount of rent-free land on which a *maṭh* was built and a tank was excavated by the royal order. In 1464 he died in this very *maṭh*. According to his followers Viṣṇusvāmī the famous Vaiṣṇava teacher was a disciple of their master, and the temple on his (Nām-dev's) tomb was built by the joint efforts of his disciples like Viṣṇusvāmī, Vohardās, Jallo and Laḍḍā. Vohardāsa's descendants are now the teachers of the sect and they look after the administration of the *maṭh*, which includes giving relief to the poor from the income of the temple. Members of the sect of Bābā Nām-dev in the district of

Gurudāspur too are mostly descendants of Vohardās. In the Ghomān *maṭh* there is a two hundred years old manuscript known to be containing words of Nām-dev. This work written in Hindī with a sprinkling of Marāṭhī is considered as sacred as the Granth Sāhib of the Sikhs. But to the Nām-devites *kripāns* are not sacred, and in their temple they do not touch this weapon.

Nām-dev's birth is celebrated on the Śrī-pañchamī day; and during the first two days of the month of Māgha as well as in the Janmāṣṭamī day annual fairs take place in Ghomān. But the fair in the month of Māgha attract the largest number of people. Nām-dev's sayings have been included in the Granth Sāhib. This famous person has two less known namesakes. One of them was a calico-printer by profession and had his place in Buland Shahar. Nām-dev of Mārwāṛ was a cotton-carder by birth. Both these were reputed as *bhaktas* and have numerous devoted followers.

Besides these, there are many *bhaktas* in the Mahārāṣṭra and it is not possible to mention them all in this short lecture. But in spite of this handicap there remains a name which has an urgent claim on our attention. It is the able Rām-dās Svāmī, the guru of the famous Śivājī. In his royal disciple Rām-dās met an excellent champion for the re-establishment of the religious ideal of the Hindus. But, pledged though he was for the protection and advancement of his own religion Śivājī had every regard for Islam and was never half-hearted as regards discharging his duties towards saints and shrines of the same faith.

From the Mahārāṣṭra, let us now turn to Gujarat. The name that deserves to be mentioned first is Narsī Mehtā (1413-1476) who was born in a Nāgar Brāhmaṇ family of Junāgaṛ. Beautiful songs of divine love that he composed are a permanent source of joy and inspiration to the *bhaktas* of Gujarat, Saurāṣṭra, Cutchh and the neighbouring places.

Besides Narsī Mehtā there are other *bhaktas* too: one of them is a goldsmith Akhā Bhagat (1613-1663) who flourished in Ahmedabad. In the beginning he was a Vaiṣṇava but turned, later on, a follower of Vedānta. He left behind considerable number of songs composed by him. Niṣkulānanda (born in 1775) another *bhakta*—was an inhabitant of Gaṛhṛā Kāṭhiāwāṛ. He was a carpenter by birth. After his initiation into the Svāmī-Nārāyaṇī sect he composed some very excellent songs.

Santa Rām a well known *sādhaka* of Gujarat lived and preached in Nadiād. In Umreṭh and Pādrā too there are two centres of his followers who do not worship any image. Mussulmans too are allowed to enter this sect.

Mādhavgar (*circa* 1824) flourished in the neighbourhood of Nadiād. He did not like sectarianism and preached a very liberal teaching which was as free from any distinctive mark as the *Brahman* itself. He had little regard for conventional ideas and practices, and he said that no effort for spiritual uplift could succeed without lofty principles and practice of morality. In Gujarat there are many *sādhakas* who follow Lakṣmaṇgar.[8]

*Sādhakas* of the Svāmī-Nārāyaṇī sect like Brahmānanda, Devānanda and others created even among the Mussulmans, and Hindus of the Pariah class, an interest for the spiritual life. By their efforts the message of Divine Love was spread even among the lowliest.

We now come to Tulsī-dās one of the

most famous religious teachers of the Northern India. Born in a Kanaujiā Brāhmaṇ family of Rājpur (Bāndā), he had his initiation in the cult of Bhakti, it is said, in the unorthodox sect of Rāmānanda and was sixth in succession from that famous teacher. Rāmānanda was the most successful among those who tried to impart vigour and fulness to Indian religious life by holding before people a perfectly ideal Rāma and Krisṇa. Number of North Indian people who have quenched their spiritual thirst by reading Tulsīdās's Hindī Rāmāyaṇ can scarcely be estimated. To many of them, even the Rāmāyaṇa of Vālmīki is of less value than the Rāmcharitmānas which is overflowing, as it were, with a divine love and holiness. Tulsīdās's Vinaya-patrikā, which contains some excellent prayers, is also a priceless gem to the *bhaktas*.

Tulsīdās's Rāmāyaṇ calls to our mind the authors of the Bengali Rāmāyaṇ and Mahābhārat. A detailed account of them is however needless to a Bengali audience. But, a matter of common knowledge though it is how Krittivās's Rāmāyaṇ and Kāśīrām-dās's Mahābhārat have kept every Bengali home lively for the last few centuries, very few are aware of the interesting fact that Kāśīrām-dās's Mahābhārat has reached the hand of the Hindī speaking peasants in the far away districts of Rāypur and Bilāspur (C.P.) During his tour over those districts the lecturer has actually seen this book read by the people. As can easily be imagined they do not understand the language well but like Tulsī-Rāmāyaṇ every day they read carefully a portion of their Kāśīdāsī Mahābhārat.

Not only in Bengal but also in other parts of India, authors of the vernacular versions of the Rāmāyaṇa and the Mahābhārata have done immense service to the Hindu religion and culture. But the Mahābhārata, thanks to Kāśirāmdās, has nowhere been made so popular as it has been in Bengal. Side by side with the vernacular version of national epics various popular institutions such as *yātrā*, *kathakatā*, pilgrimage, religious fairs, *bhajans*, *kīrtans*, and *saṃkīrtan* etc. helped greatly towards keeping India religiously alive.

Nothing has yet been spoken about the Śaiva devotees. Though Śaiva or Nakulīśa Pāśupata scriptures were available among the Kashmirian scholars, real Śaiva *bhaktas* however were to be found in the Southern India. The famous expositors of the Śaiva philosophy were the Kashmirian Abhinava-gupta of the eleventh century, and his predecessors like Siddha Somānanda and others. But a treatment of the Śaiva philosophy as well as the Pratyabhijñā śāstra of Abhinava will be out of place in this lecture. And these were not popular things. For, those *sādhakas* who were devotionally minded cared little for the abstruse works of Utpalāchārya who wrote for the learned, and turned profitably to the simple utterances of Śaiva *bhaktas*.

Śaivism had its stronghold in Kashmir where its different schools such as Suprabheda Āgama, Svāyambhuva Āgama, and Vīra Śaiva Āgama were prevalent. In a work named the Channavasava-purāṇa names of many Śaiva bhaktas, legendary as well as historical, are available.

In the Southern India too, as in Kashmir, Śaiva *bhaktas* or Nāyanmārs cared little for learned treatises. Works like the Siddhānta-śikhāmaṇi, the Aṣṭāviṃśati Śaivāgama or the writings of Utpalāchārya or Mariton̩ṭa dārya were handled exclusively by scholars. From the Śiva-jñāna-bodha (1223) of Meikaṇḍadeva we learn that most of the Śaiva *bhaktas* were non-Brāhmaṇs. This author was a Śaiva teacher who worked among the masses. After him Tiru Jñāna Sambandha wrote his Śaiva-samaya-neri, and in the beginning of the fourteenth century Umāpati Śivāchārya wrote his Śivaprakāśa. But more important than these were the preachings of non-Brāhmaṇ Śiva-vākya, Pattinātthu Pille, Paran Jyothi Munivār, Aghora Śivāchārya, Śiva yoga Gyāni. They were against the three things: Brāhmaṇ, idols and customs prescribed in the *śāstras*. According to them one cannot be religious by a blind observance of the rules of conduct given in ancient books, and the religious life was a matter of direct personal experience and it has seldom any connection with the narrow conception of the Divinity in any material image.

Śivavākya of the seventeenth century says: "What can be done by these artificial gods whose honour and even existence are under human control? How can they bring salvation to me? What is the use, then, of arranging flowers near a block of stone, and what benefit accrues from the burning of incense, and the sounding of bells before an idol and from circumambulating it and observing similar other practices? In the same way, vain is the observance of ninety-six rules by the Yogī and the incarceration of the flesh, the muttering of *mantras*, pilgrimage to holy places and bathing in the Ganges. So give up attachment and pacify the mind; the holy Benares will rise up in your heart. It is the ideal Divinity and not the artificial image that is to be worshipped."

Bhadiragiriār very humbly surrenders himself to God with the following words: "When, O Lord, will my senses be curbed, my pride turned down and my struggles be ended in an excellent repose?" He then doubts if it is possible to realise God by a study of the scriptures, and to develop *bhakti* by an extensive reading, and looks for a day when he will be able to burn the scriptures and set the Vedas at naught and the door of his own inner self will be open unto the Supreme Bliss. For his spiritual freedom he becomes impatient. "When," askes he, "will freedom come to me who am like an imprisoned fish, and when shall I be able to lay myself at the feet of God and merge my own nature into His?"

Pattinātthu Pille says that God does not reside in a stone or copper image which is made by human hands and is also subject to occasional cleansing. "Look for him," says, Pattinātthu, "in the inmost recess of your heart, in the heaven of *sādhaka's* soul and in the love of humanity." Nothing could be deeper and more elevating.

It is very difficult to have a complete historical account of all Indian *bhaktas* in any single book. G o k u l-n ā t h (fl. in 1568) the son of Viṭṭhal wrote a work named C h a u-r ā ś ī v ā r t t ā or the Eightyfour Messages. And next comes the B h a k t a m ā l of N ā b h ā who is supposed to have lived about the sixteenth century. This Nābhā as an orphan of the Ḍom (undertaker) caste was picked up by A g r a-d ā s of the Vallabha sect who brought him up.[9] Some believe that Nābhā belonged to the sect of Rāmānanda and this was the reason of his paying additional attention to the worshippers of Rām. But in his commentary to the Bhaktamāl P r i y ā-d ā s has referred to many *bhaktas* of Krisṇa as well. The reason of this is to be found in the fact that the commentator belonged to the Krisṇite Brahma sect founded by Mādhva.

In the Bhaktamāl there are accounts of one hundred and sixty *bhaktas*. Except some twenty names which are legendary we find that all other *bhaktas* are historical. But the Bhaktamāl deals mainly with *bhaktas* who are sectarians and pay respect to the *śāstras*. An exception however has been made in case of Ravi-dās and Kabīr. Though they did not belong to high castes their prominence among the disciples of Rāmānanda has made it impossible that their names should be left out of any chronicle of *bhaktas* worth the name. But names like Dādū, Nānak and Rajjab are wanting in the Bhaktamāl. The cause of such an indifference on the part of the authors of the work, who were sectarians, is that they were much afraid of extending recognition to the latter group of *bhaktas* who were extremely frank about their denunciation of sects. That the South Indian *bhaktas* have not been mentioned in the Bhaktamāl is probably due to ignorance on the part of the author. But fortunately for us there are Bhaktamāls other than that composed by Nābhā. These and similar biographical materials preserved in different *maṭhs* and sectarian head-quarters when properly collected will furnish the basis of an excellent history of the *sādhakas* of the Mediæval India. It is needless to discuss here about all the *bhaktas* of the orthodox type mentioned in the Bhaktamāl. For, this work is easily available and those who care for the subject may have a look into it. Besides the above there are some documents written in Persian. Among them all, the Dabistān has been utilised by Wilson in his work on Indian religions. On Tamil *bhaktas* too there are works which have been mentioned earlier in this lecture. The lecturer earnestly hopes that young Indian seekers of truth will collect and study all such documents and help towards giving a complete account of India's efforts in the field of religious and spiritual culture.

## LECTURE II.

# LIBERAL THINKERS

A quest of the origin of the heterodox religious sects of the Indian Mediæval times will carry one to an age vastly anterior to that period. Referring to this the Bāüls say that only the artificial religions have an historical beginning, while the religion which is natural and free, is as old as the time itself. And these very words find an echo in the Sahajānanda of Sundar-dās (born in 1596) who was a disciple of Dādū. The Bāüls further say that the natural religion professed by them goes even beyond the Vedic times (*circa* 2000 B.C.), and the Vrātyas mentioned in the Atharva-Veda were the Bāüls of their own days. But it is scarcely of any use to give emphasis on a probable connexion with the pre-historic times. *Sādhakas* like Kabīr, Dādū, and Rajjab also spoke of the natural religion as a thing eternal. Earlier still, the teachers of the Nāth and Yogī sects who flourished in Bengal, Nepal and other parts of the North-Eastern India and whose history preceded the Mahomedan occupation of India by several centuries, were to a great extent free from the bondage of the *śāstras*.[10] Influence which *sādhakas* of these schools, such as Gorakhnāth, Mīnanāth and the Siddhas, exercised upon their successors in different parts of India has not been inconsiderable. Even the teachings of Kabīr, Nānak and similar other saints bear unmistakeable marks of this influence. Songs of Mainămatī and Gopīchānd which were contributions of the Nāth and Yogī sects of Bengal were broadcasted all over India by the itinerant Yogī singers called Bharatharis. The present lecturer has heard the song of Gopīchānd in distant places like the Punjab, N.-W. Frontier Province, Sindh, Cutchh, Gujarat, the Mahārāṣṭra and Karṇātak. As investigations about the history of the Nāth and Yogī sects have begun we shall not here go into details about them.

The Nirañjan sect as well as the religious movements of the North-Eastern India had considerable influence on all the schools of religious reformers of the Indian Midland. These too have been discussed by competent persons and are still being discussed; so we may well leave out this subject.

The Nirañjan sect still maintains its influence in Orissa, and its religious teachings travelled thence to the Midland and the Eastern part of India where it has not lost its force even at the present times.[11] From the sayings of Kabīr and other saints we can infer that the teachings of the Nirañjan sect was once very popular in Rajputana and the North-Western Punjab. Teachings of the Nāth, Yogī and Nirañjan sects are still not dead in the North-Western India, Jodhpur, Cutchh, Sindh and neighbouring places. *Maṭhs* and holy shrines of the twelve branches of the Yogī sect which are situated in different parts of India are a standing testimony to the great influence which the sect once exercised on the religious life of India.

Among the radical religious reformers of Mediæval India, Rāmānanda (*circa* 1370-1440) stands foremost. He is the veritable redeemer of this age.

From the Haribhakti-prakāśikā —a commentary on the Bhaktamāl—written by Rāmānuj-dās Harivar (1857-1864) we learn that Viṣṇu-citta and Śaṭhakopa were among those who by their teaching inspired Rāmānuja with *prema* and *bhakti*. These two teachers belonged to a very low stratum of the society. So we can easily assume that Rāmānuja was liberal to a very great extent, but in spite of this his followers of successive generations reverted to observation of traditional customs. In their cooking, dining, drawing water and drinking it, and regarding the touch of other people, Rāmānuja's followers are now-a-days such scrupulous observers of minute rules that they are generally known to be very orthodox.

According to Harivara, Rāmānanda was a follower of Rāmānuja and fifth in succession from the master. But when urged by true *bhakti* he travelled widely all over India, he did not care to maintain the orthodox standard of conduct. On account of this lapse on his part he had to go out of the sect, although he occupied at that time a very high position among the followers of Rāmānuja. Rāmānanda realised that for him who had taken to the path of *bhakti*, rules of caste and various other worldly rules had become meaningless. So he could easily accept food from any one "In the orthodox society *gotras* are known by the names of *riṣis*. If such a thing is permissible why should not all mankind be known by the name of the Great God who is worshipped by all such *riṣis*? And as regards the social position it should be decided by the excellence of *bhakti* and not by birth."

Thus, from his artificial height Rāmānanda descended to the natural field of *prema* and *bhakti* and began to preach his spiritual doctrines to all people irrespective of their caste and creed.

His teachings, delivered in Hindī instead of Sanskrit, was saved from the fate of being an exclusive property of scholars or the high caste people. By preaching in vernacular Rāmānanda could call together all people to the natural festive ground of the spiritual culture. And this gave a great impetus to the Hindī Literature.

The following twelve are known to be chief disciples of Rāmānanda.[12] 1. Ravi-dās (shoe-maker), 2. Kabīr (Mahomedan weaver), 3. Dhannā (Jāṭh), 4. Senā (barbar), 5. Pīpā (Rājput), 6. Bhavānanda, 7. Sukhānanda, 8. Āśānanda, 9. Sur-surānanda, 10. Paramānanda, 11. Mahānanda, 12. Śrī-ānanda.

So we see that there are in Rāmānanda's sect, *bhaktas* from various castes. There is a tradition among the *bhaktas* that the disciples mentioned in the latter part of the list joined Rāmānanda from the sect of Rāmānuja. But besides these twelve Rāma-nanda had many more disciples most of whom came from the lower strata of the society. There were women too among his disciples. According to Rāmānanda any *bhakta* taking shelter in God merges his previous identity in Him. Hence he is no longer different from his brother *bhakta* who might have come from a so-called higher caste. But in spite of this, the orthodox writers of the Bhaktamāl and other works accepted as truth those foolish stories which depict Rāmānanda as the unwilling initiator of Kabīr who belonged to a low caste. If we accept these stories as authentic history we are at a loss to account for so many of his other disciples who were far from being of a high caste. On this point there are interesting accounts in the literature of the Ravidāsī and other sects. We regret that they cannot be quoted for want of time. From his sayings preserved in the Granth Sāhib of the Sikhs we learn how Rāmānanda said: "Why do you any longer call me to go to the temple? Him, omnipresent and all-pervading, I have met in the very temple of my heart." In spite of the clear import of such sayings some foreign critics do not like to admit that Rāmānanda gave up all regard for image-worship and the rules of caste.[13] The argument in support of their view is that the present day followers of Rāmānanda, that is, those who believe that they follow the master, worship images and observe caste. But following a similar line of argument one can say that the Lord Jesus, an incarnation of mercy and non-violence, was not what he is usually known to be, because of his professed followers, the high priests of the cult of imperialism which promotes violence either in the shape of exploiting weaker races or in the shape of armed conflicts among various gangs of such exploiters. To judge the past solely by the standard of the present is a bad critical method.

Rāmānanda in accordance with the practice of his day retained the use of the name Rām as indicating the Deity. To him God is one, loving, omniscient and is not the attributeless *Brahman* but a person, a loving friend after his own heart, a personal God.

This mystic attitude awakened all true seekers of God whether within his own sect or outside it. The tradition has summerised this fact by the following couplet:

*Bhakti Drāviṛ upajī lāye Rāmānand |*
*pragaṭ kiyo Kabīr-ne sapta-dvip nau-khaṇḍ ||*

"*Bhakti* arose among the Dravidians (in the South); Rāmānanda carries it (to the North) and Kabīr spreads it all over (the Earth, which consists of) the seven continents and is divided into nine parts."

Next important names to be mentioned after Rāmānanda are those of the *bhaktas* Sadan and Nāmdev. Sadan was a butcher by profession. A fine story about him given in the Bhaktamāl is as follows: Sadan had a *śālgrām* by which he weighed the raw meat to be sold. This attracting the notice of a pious man who felt distressed at the sad plight of the symbol of Viṣṇu and asked Sadan for the *śālgrām.* Sadan readily satisfied this stranger's desire. But in the night following the new owner of the *śālgrām* dreamt to his utter surprise that the god was desiring to be put back with Sadan whose simple *bhakti* was fascinating. It goes without saying that the pious man had to fulfill the desire of the perverse god.

The Bhaktamāl gives an account of how Sadan through various trials, physical as well as emotional, advanced in spiritual life and was finally called by Jagannāth of Puri to that deity's seat. There are two of Sadan's songs in the Granth Sāhib of the Sikhs. Besides this famous Sadan there was in Sindh about 1400 another saintly namesake of his who was a butcher too. We have referred to Nāmdev in our first lecture. Like Rāmānanda he too carried the Bhakti cult of the South to the North. The fact that many of the devotional songs composed by Nāmdev have been included in the Granth Sāhib of the Sikhs is a measure of the great influence he had once on the spiritual life of the Northern Hindustan.

There are some important names among the disciples of Rāmānanda besides the twelve principal ones already referred to. One of them is Anantādand whose *maṭh* is still in existence in Galtā near Āmer (Jaypur). His disciple Krisṇadās was born in Kullu in the Himalayas. The ruling chief of Āmer was first a follower of the Yogī sect but subsequently he turned a disciple of Krisṇadās.

Agra-dās and Kīlha, the two disciple of Krisṇa-dās Pai-ahari, were excellent poets. Many among the *bhaktas*, such as Keval-rām, Harinārāyaṇ, Padmanābh, Gadādhar, Dev-dās, Kalyāṇ-dās belong to this section of the Rāmānanda's followers. The following sayings of Agra-dās are very popular among the *bhaktas*:

"Worship the Lord God who is the god of all gods."

"Days that pass away in joy and bliss constitute the fruition of life."

"To attain Hari" says Agra-dās, "lose your body and mind (in Him)."

Nābhā was a disciple of this Agra-dās. As a child, Nābhā was forsaken by his widowed mother who was a Ḍom woman and had scarcely any means for bringing up her son. Agra-dās brought up this orphan and developed in him a new vision. With a view to conceal this humble birth of Nābhā some have traced his genealogy to Hanumān the great monkey-god and the famous devotee. Nābhā's guru asked him to write a biographical history of the *bhaktas*; but Nābhā at first excused himself as being an illiterate person though finally he composed the Bhaktamāl after the guru had commanded him to do the work.

Priyā-dās of the Mādhvī sect who wrote a commentary to this work virtually supplemented the accounts of *bhaktas* given in it. Another commentator of the Bhaktamāl was Lāl-dās who with the assistance Vaiṣṇav-dās the grandson of Priyā-dās considerably added to our knowledge of the *bhaktas*. Lāl-dās's commentary is called the Bhakta-uravasī. Lāl-dās, an inhabitant of Kāndhel, was known earlier as Lakṣmaṇ-dās, but after accepting the the discipleship of Vallabha Lāl of the Rādhā-vallabhī sect he changed his name.

A third commentator of the Bhaktamāl was Lālā Gumānī-lāl (1761) of Rohtak. Rām-prasād (1864) of Mirpur made a much simplified version of the Bhaktamāl.

It has been mentioned before that Nābhā's Bhaktamāl does not contain any account of *sādhakas* who did not distinguish between peoples of different religious profession such as the Hindus and the Mussulmans and it does not contain any account of Nānak, Dādū and Rajjab etc. But fortunately for us there are, besides Nābhā's work, Bhaktamāls written by a number of *bhaktas* such as Rāghav-dās and others. Many biographical accounts of *bhaktas* preserved in *maṭhs* and places associated with *sādhus*, also add to our knowledge of unorthodox saintly lives.

Kīlha the fellow-disciple of Agra-dās was the son of Sumer-dev who was the *subedar* of Gujarat. Coming to know of him the wellknown Rājā Mānsiṅgh had an interview with this holy man in Mathurā and was very much astonished at his spiritual elevation.

The K h ā k ī sect claim their origin from Kīlha. Members of this sect have their centres in Oudh, Jaipur, Farrukhābād, and Hanumāngaṛ.

After giving an account of the less important disciples of Rāmānanda let us turn to his twelve principal disciples.

R a v i-d ā s was born of cobbler parents in Benares. According to the Haribhakti-prakāśikā he maintained his family by repairing shoes; but even after his spiritual illumination by Rāmānanda's grace he did not give up his profession. It is said that a *sādhu* offered him the '*sparśa-maṇi*' but he declined to accept it and said that his own small earning and the simple style of living was preferable to enormous wealth which the '*maṇi*' might easily bring.

For his spiritual exercises and for the service of the *sādhus* Ravi-dās had with great difficulty caused a *maṭh* to be built. The local Brāhmans did not like this and complained to the king that the cobbler Ravi-dās was polluting all in the name of religious life. The ruler of the land called him to the court for administering a rebuke but Ravi-dās's face beaming with a divine love charmed the king immensely and the accusations of the Brāhmans completely failed.

The story goes that the queen J h ā l ī of Chitore became a disciple of Ravi-dās. This naturally vexed the Brāhmans who complained about this to the king. The king asked Ravi-dās as well as the Brāhman clique to substantiate their claim to be a guru. The Brāhmans, then, began to recite Vedas but the king was not satisfied with their performance and Ravi-dās who chanted his simple *bhajans* won the heart of the king.

There is a legend that at the request of the queen Jhālī Ravi-dās was present in a *Yajña* (Vedic sacrifice). The Brāhmans did not like this and probably to remind Ravi-dās of his humble birth they said that they would not eat anything cooked at the place of the *Yajña.* But when after cooking their own food in different places they all sat down to take their food they found to their astonishment that between every two of them one Ravi-dās was taking his meal. That the queen of Chitore was a disciple of Ravi-dās may be said to give plausibility to the tradition current among the *bhaktas* that M ī r ā-b ā ī was a disciple of his.

More than thirty among Ravi-dās's *bhajans* which are full of divine love and earnest longing for the Lord, have been included into the Granth Sāhib.

Ravi-dās says:

> "Rām that has engrossed the attention of the common people is not the Rām which I seek."
>
> "In every object Thou art existing all the while. It is my fault that I have not learnt to see Thee with my own eyes."
>
> "Tired is my mind after wandering in His quest. No longer can I continue in this profitless venture."
>
> "Him, for whose sake I have wandered far far away, I have discovered at this moment in my own humble frame."

On the futility of reading the scriptures or the Vedas as a means of satisfying one's great longing for God, Ravi-dās says:

> "The recitation of the Vedic *mantras* even for many millions of times will not satisfy the pangs of that longing."

About the sublime nature of his mystic communion with God Ravi-dās says:

> "The pure flavour of it is unique and has neither any origin nor any des-

> truction. It is past and yet not past; it does not decay and it is existent within every being."

This experience holds before Ravi-dās a new vision of the world. He says:

> "Wherever I go I see that Thy adoration is constantly going on."

Ravi-dās was ever ready to give service to others. Whenever any meeting of the *sādhus* took place or they all went to any place of pilgrimage Ravi-dās came to serve them. Young people with whom he was very popular gave, under Ravi-dās's leadership, various service to others. This naturally displeased their guardians who charged Ravi-dās with spoiling their wards who in course of serving the people came to lose their orthodox view of life. While he served others Ravi-dās prayed to God and made obeisance to Him. Some songs which he composed for these occasions are of unique charm.

Such was Ravi-dās of whom the leather-workers all over India are proud. And they do not, of course, fail to profess to be followers of this great saint.

Senā who was a barber by caste received new life by the grace of Rāmānanda. Even after attaining this new life of the *bhakta*,

Senā continued in his professional work. The king in whose service Senā was, as soon as he learned about the saintliness of his barber, made him his guru. Senā was an inhabitant of Bāndhogar. Even now, Senā's descendants are revered by the ruling chiefs of the place. In the Granth Sāhib there is a Saina *bhajan* or a *bhajan* by Senā.

Bhavānanda (*circa* 1400) was a scholar. By Rāmānanda's order he wrote the Amrit-dhār which explains for ordinary people the doctrines of Vedānta in the simple Hindī of his day.

Dhannā said to have been born in 1415 was a Jāṭh. In his boyhood he received instruction from a Brāhman. Even from that time he felt that he enjoyed everything as a loving sharer of God. When Dhannā wanted more lofty teaching from his Brāhman *guru* he was asked to go to Rāmānanda in Benares. Rāmānanda gladly accepted Dhannā as his disciple though the latter was of a humble birth.

Dhannā's peasant comrades asked him, how he benefited by turning to *bhakti*, and told him that better than *bhakti* would have been agriculture which might have brought in ten times of what he sowed. To this Dhannā replied, that the field to which he had then turned was giving him a return which was a thousand times of what he sowed. Three *bhajans* in *rāg* Āśā and one in *rāg* Dhānaśrī composed by Dhannā have been included in the Granth Sāhib.

Pīpā (said to have been born in 1425) was a Rājput by birth. He was the ruler of Gāmrohagaṛ in Rajputana. Originally he was a Śākta but as he received from Rāmānanda the teachings of *bhakti* he renounced his kingdom. At the time of his leaving the palace his queens begged to accompany him. But Pīpā refused to take them along with him. Rāmānanda however interposed and said that Pīpā had no right to refuse them permission to accompany him if the queens were ready to renounce their royal splendour and to follow him in an ordinary life. On this condition one only was found to accompany Pīpā and that was his youngest queen Sītā.

There is a story that eager to meet Krisṇa, Pīpā leaped into sea and met the Lord and that meeting was attested by a mark in his body. The custom that obtains in Pīpā's *maṭh* in Dwārakā of putting the mark of a seal of Krisṇa on the body of *bhaktas* goes back to this story.

Pīpā was very kind to the poor. It is said that once on his way to Dwārakā he met his devoted admirer Chidhar or Śrīdhar Bhakta. This extremely poor man sold his own *dhoti* for offering food to his master. Pīpā and his wife, when they came to know of this, felt much distressed. Then, for collecting money to relieve the poor man Sītā sang and danced to the accompaniment of her husband's *sāreṅgī*. This brought in some money which the saintly couple had the satisfaction of giving for the relief of the poor *bhakta*.

In Pīpāvaṭ which lies on the way to Dwārakā there is a big *maṭh* of Pīpā. This is very well-known for its hospitality. There is one *bhajan* in Dhānaśrī *rāg* composed by Pīpā, which has been included into the Granth Shāhib. His songs are very often heard in the religious festivals of the Sikh *sādhus*.

Sukhānand was, by nature, a loving heart with devotional bent of mind. So he accompanied Rāmānanda at his renouncement of Rāmānuja's sect. It is believed that Sukhānanda's fore-fathers were followers of the Tantra. This is the reason why his works are sometimes called the Bhakti-Tantra. He remained constantly engaged in praying to God. At the bidding of guru he did all sorts of things but at the same time repeated the name of God always during his work, and the emotion suffiused his eyes with tears. Thus he made successive activities his chaplet. Sukhānanda's utterances are greatly prized by the *sādhakas*.

After his contact with Rāmānanda, Sur-surānanda began a new life and for realising his ideal unhampered he severed all connection with the world. His wife (whose name according to the Haribhaktiprakāśikā was Surasari-jī) however wanted to follow him in his path of spiritual betterment, but Sur-surānanda did not like this and prevented her from doing so. But on her report to the guru Rāmānanda, the latter asked Sur-surānanda the reason of his refusal and suggested that a woman like her who was devoted to her husband and had faith in his ideal could well be made a comrade in *sādhanā*. Sur-surānanda excused that a young and beautiful woman like her might invite danger and worry from the outside. "You are a man", said Ramānanda then, "and are to give her protection from all sorts of danger by your manly prowess; and it would be sheer unmanliness to leave this responsibility for somebody else." Hence Sur-surānanda had to go for *sādhanā* accompanied by his wife. Some scoundrels belonging to the Mussulman sect tried to molest this saintly couple but they according to the story were overpowered by God who assumed a terrible shape for the protection of his *bhakta*.

The most important among the disciples of Rāmānanda was Kabīr whose superior spiritual achievements came to have a sovereign influence on the people of the Indian Mediæval times. Kabīr's influence, direct or indirect, on all liberal religious movements that occurred in the Mediæval times after him, is uncommonly deep. According to the author of the Kabīr-kasauṭī Kabīr's death occurred in 1518. It is said that he was born in 1398 and lived to his 120th year. Western scholars accept this date of his demise but not of birth. Hunter says that Kabīr lived between 1300 and 1420 while according to Beal, Kabīr lived till 1490. Some Christian missionaries accepting the date of Kabīr's death (1518) as given in the Kasauṭi believed that he lived between 1440 and 1518. But Babu Shyām-sundar Dās of the Nāgarī Prachāriṇī Sabhā has acquired an old manuscript of Kabīr's sayings said to be dated 1504. If the missionaries are to be considered right this manuscript becomes a contemporary document but on examination of the text printed from this manuscript one becomes sceptical about its early date. This suspicion is corroborated by the evidence of the Bhārat Brāhmaṇ which gives 1398 and 1448 as the date of Kabīr's birth and death. Dr. Führer's researches also support this evidence. In his Monumental Antiquities and Inscriptions in the North Western Provinces and Oudh Dr. Führer has described Kabīr's *rauza* in Khirnī in Basti on the river Amī. This *rauza* was built by Bijli Khān in 1450 and was repaired by Nawab Fidai Khan in 1567. This testifies to the genuineness of the account given in the Bhārat Brāhmaṇ. Immediately after the death of Kabīr, Bijli Khan built a temple on Kabīr's tomb in Magahar, and the *rauza* mentioned above followed two years after. This shows well how greatly Kabīr influenced the heart of the Mussulman *sādhakas*.

It is beyond doubt that Kabīr was the son of a Mahomedan weaver (Jolā) but the Hindu writers, such as the author of the Bhaktamāl and its several commentaries, tried their best to conceal this historical fact. That Kabīr was a Jolā finds corroboration in his sayings, and his name points to his Mahomedan origin. Still to get over these difficulties some Hindu writers would assert that, though brought up in a Mahomedan family, Kabīr was originally the son of a Brāhman.* There are, besides these, other Hindu writers less critical who would solemnly claim that Kabīr being but the Eternal Spirit embodying truth and clear vision, was never born of a mortal. The Eternal Being in a sportive mood lay on a lotus in the lake of Lahar-talāo near Benares and a Jolā couple picked him and brought him up as their child.

It is useless to discuss these obvious absurdities. From records preserved among the followers of Dādū (Kabīr's disciple) and the testimony of other documents it is clear that Kabīr was born of Jolā parents. Ābul Fazl and the author of the Dabistān too attest

* According to some, Rāmānanda was not originally willing to initiate the low born Kabīr but the latter managed to plant himself before the guru's door very early in the morning when Rāmānanda stepped out and at the touch of the Mahomedan weaver uttered 'Rāma, Rāma' in repugance. This 'Rāma, Rāma', Kabīr accepted as his *mantra* and thus ingratiated himself in Rāmānanda's favour. This story is ludicrously absurd; for most of Rāmānanda's disciples were people of humble origin and had no such story of their first contact with the guru.

to his Mahomedan origin. In their opinion Kabīr strictly speaking was not a Mussulman in his faith but he was a *Muwahhid* or an unitarian theistic *bhakta*. Thus Kabīr was doubtless the son of a Mahomedan weaver but his forefathers were among the early converts from Hinduism to Islam. From the lot of such converts in general during Mahomedan times it is to be gathered that conversion did not improve them intellectually and spiritually. Illiteracy and want of education still reigned supreme among them. It appears that God, simply to glorify His truth, has reared such a great personage among persons of a very humble rank. The fact is that these people were not at all burdened by the weight of the traditions of the past, and hence were free to see for themselves. Kabīr got a new consciousness from the teachings of Rāmānanda which gave him initiation of the spiritual life. Castes, idols, pilgrimage, austerities and outward symbols of religious life he shunned completely and struck a very hard blow at the root of various superstitions. The short extent of this lecture unfortunately forbids us to illustrate all these by quotation from his sayings. Even after his initiation Kabīr went about meeting *bhaktas* and wise men of both Hindu and Mahomedan communities and having talks with them. He had an intimacy with the Sūfis. Among them he had a very close contact with Shaikh Takki who belonged to the Suhrawardi branch of the Sūfis.

Though initiated into a spiritual life Kabīr was married; the name of his wife was Loī and the name of his son and daughter was Kamāl and Kamālī respectively. Kamālī was married to a Brāhman husband. The present day followers of Kabīr are not very willing to admit these facts. Kamāl too was a *bhakta* and a man of deep spiritual experience. He was also a poet of a very high order. Some stray fragments of his composition, which are available among *sādhus*, are of marvellous beauty. On the death of his father, Kamāl was asked by people to organise the sect of his father's followers. He rejected the idea and said that such an act on his part would be nothing short of killing the truth uttered by his father, and the killing of father's truth would be tentamount to killing the father himself spiritually. Kamāl thus refused the rank of a parricide. This however displeased many of Kabīr's followers. "Kamāl's birth", they opined, "made an end of Kabīr's line."

These words however are capable of a different interpretation. Kabīr's followers Dādū, Rajjab and many others were also married and according to them married life only was a complete life. This shows that Kabīr had not much respect for a monastic life which was at best an incomplete life.

Kabīr's sayings giving his doctrine became available in later times in two principal recensions. One of these known as the Vījak was made the basis of his sect by Surat Gopāl who established his centre in Benares. Influenced by the spirit of Benares, members of this sect gradually showed increased leaning towards scholastic writings, especially Vedānta literature, and to monastic life. The famous commentator of the Vijak was Viśvanāth Siṅgh the ruler of Bhāgelkhaṇḍ State, which gave its name to the commentary.

Dharam-dās the Bānia disciple of Kabīr went to over to Chhattisgaṛ and established another sect of Kabīr. Members of this sect read the master's sayings in that recension which include, besides the Vījak, collections like Kabīr-sāgar and give importance to the Trijyā commentary of the Vījak. Dharam-dās was a married man and assumed his spiritual career with his wife. In this branch of Kabīr's followers gurus are required to be married men and are succeeded by their sons. Their chief *maṭh* has been shifted from Kudarmal (Chhattisgaṛ) and is now in Dāmākheṛā. Very recently the last *Mahānta* of the *maṭh* has died without any male child.

Of the two sects following Kabīr the Chhattisgaṛī sect is more influential. According to the official version of the sect, its members are more than four millions (42 lacs). Members of the Surat-Gopālī sect, mostly to be found attached to the *maṭh* in Benares, are very scanty in number.

There is a legend that a quarrel occurred over Kabīr's funeral. For, his chief Hindu disciple Raja Vīr-siṅgh desired to cremate the master's dead body, while the Mussulman disciple Bijli Khān thought that burial would be the proper form of its disposal. But they say that a miracle made an end of this unseemly quarrel; for, on lifting the cover of the dead body only some flowers were found and no dead body. Half of these flowers were taken by the Mussulmans to be buried in Magahar while the remaining half was brought over to Benares for cremation. It is not clear why the quarrel should occur at all; for according to the Hindus too *sādhakas* when dead are not to be cremated. But the story, however impossible, is a homage to Kabīr's spirit which allowed no opportunity of quarrel between peoples of different communities.

The sayings of Kabīr, if put together, will constitute many volumes. Of course quite a great part is full of repetition, which may be original or otherwise. It might be that Kabīr said the same thing on different occasions and to different persons in different words. Or it may be that people hearing him have given slightly altered versions of these sayings. But besides these written sayings, there are others, which are very deep in their meaning and are orally transmitted by successive generations of *sādhus*.

Kabīr, who liked simple and natural living, was himself a weaver. He sold in the market the stuff he produced in his loom, and with him *sādhanā* did not mean a life divorced from ordinary physical labour. He always advocated such labour as would keep a person outside the charity of another and may at times give him a chance of offering material help to others.

Kabīr liked that everyone should earn his

livelihood and help his fellow-men. Only his earning should not end in hoarding money by fair means or foul. He was of opinion that if the money earned be always kept in circulation by using the same in philanthropic undertakings that would create no social disorder. Only when its circulation stops, money creates in society much misery and injustice. Later on Dādū, Kabīr's disciple, adopted these views in organising his Brahma-sampradāya or the Band of the Brahma.

Kabīr never accepted the meaningless formalism either of the Hindu or of the Mahomedan society. With an uncommon power he dealt his blows against the false practices of his times. There is a story that when on the occasion of the *śrāddha* of Rāmānanda, all other disciples of the guru came to Kabīr for milk, he approached the skeleton of a dead cow and begged for milk. This strange conduct of Kabīr naturally exciting comment, he very humorously remarked that a dead cow's milk would reasonably be a fit drink for a dead person.

From his boyhood onward he lived in Benares which according to Hindu belief brings one salvation as the place of one's death. To show his indifference to such a belief, some time before his death, he asked his followers to take him to a place away from Benares. He was accordingly taken to Magahar in Basti where he passed away.

In the Nirbhaya-Jñān Granth there is the story of a Mussulman wise man. Being a globe-trotter of those days he was called Jahān-gast (world-traveller). Once he came to Kabīr's place, but as he saw a pig running about in the courtyard he was going away in disgust without meeting Kabīr. Kabīr marked this and said, "Well, though a saintly man you still cherish a prejudice against this poor creature, which indeed is unclean; but is not our inner nature, too, unclean at times?" Jahān-gast felt ashamed of his own conduct.

There is another interesting story, (though it may not be historical), in the chronicles of the *bhaktas*. Once on a joint petition from the Hindus and Mussulmans who felt much aggrevied at Kabīr's extreme heterodoxy the Emperor Sekandar Shāh Lodi summoned him to the court. On his entering the court Kabīr found his accusers, the Hindu pandits as well as the Mahomedan kāzis, gathered in the complainants' box. This amused him very much, and with a loud laughter he remarked that excepting some slight mistake regarding the address things have happened all right. This annoyed the Emperor who demanded an explanation. "My object, Your Majesty," submitted Kabīr, "was the uniting of the Hindus and Mussulmans, but nobody would ever admit the possibility of such a thing. It pleases me to-day to see that it has become possible. But if it could have occurred under the throne of an earthly sovereign like Your Majesty, could not a far wider place for the purpose have been available under the throne of the Lord of this universe. If it is possible through hatred, is it not all the more possible through love? Is not love more accommodating than hatred?" The Lodi emperor was ashamed that he believed in the charge against Kabīr and ordered him to be let off. But curiously enough according to Ferishta this emperor ordered one Brāhman to be executed for his religious difference with the Kāzi Pila Shaikh Bud. The offence of Budan, for that was the name of the Brāhman, was that he said that all religions were equal in the sight of God.

Kabīr's sayings betray deep influence

from the sects of Gorakhnāth, Nāth-panth, Nirañjan-panth, Vaiṣṇavism and Brahma-doctrine. The traditional story about Kabīr's discourse with Gorakhnāth has possibly been based on his discourse with a follower of Gorakhnāth. Kabīr's discourses with *sādhakas* of all sects have been preserved among his followers.

Simple speech was a great power with Kabīr. Effusions of his simple heart have been expressed in a very simple language which was the Hindī of those days. Not being a scholar he did not care for Sanskrit and thus he says:

"O Kabīr, Sanskrit is the water of the well, while spoken languages (*bhāṣā*) are water of the running stream."

With a thirst for discourse and communion with *sādhakas* of different ideals Kabīr travelled widely over India, and in places like Puri he stayed for quite a long time.

According to the Kabīr Mansūr Kabīr met *sādhakas* of places such as Mecca, Bagdad, Samarkand and Bokhara. In those days Bagdad was a famous centre of liberal ideas.

During his visit to Gujarat Kabīr met two brothers Tattva and Jīva on the bank of the Narmadā. There is a very big banian tree there. It occupies a big island near the Śuklatīrtha nearly thirteen miles away from Baroach on the Narmadā. There is a story that this tree was dead and withered at that time, but at the touch of Kabīr it blossomed into new life.

Kabīr was never prepared to admit that antiquity in any way guaranteed truth which was acceptable to him only after a proper examination. For this purpose he had a certain method which he has left in his 'words of test' (*parakh-vāṇī*). Besides these he has sayings that give rules of conduct, which one is to follow in striving after spiritual life. For the guidance of spiritual efforts Kabīr has left his sayings on *sādhanā* and truth. The *sādhaka* reaches his final stage in Divine love, and hence Kabīr has his sayings on this love too. If the time-limit of this lecture did not stand in our way, we might have given quotations from Kabīr's sayings to show their depth and sweetness. We must be satisfied, however, with giving here the essence of his teaching which is as follows:

If you care for truth and spiritual life, get over all artificial hindrances; be true to your own self, and be natural. For, truth is natural and simple; you need not look for it in the external world. It is not to be found in vows, garbs, rituals, pilgrimage and sectarianism. Truth remains within. One is to find it out by love, devotion and charity. Do not cherish ill-will towards any one; do not hurt any one; for, God dwells in every creature. The same God is earnestly sought after in all religions which differ only in naming Him. This makes futile all religious quarrels that go on between Hindus and Mussulmans and all other religions; so give up *ego* and vanity, and shun artificiality and untruth, and considering everyone as your own self, fill up your heart with Divine love and devotion. Then your *sādhanā* will be crowned with success. This life is an ephemeral thing. So without losing time in vain pursuits seek shelter with God. You need not seek Him in the external world; for He is within your heart where you will find Him easily. Otherwise, you will tire yourself out by treading the path of the scriptures, holy places, rituals and logic.

Kabīr was not for the mortification of the flesh. He believed that by living a natural life, in a pure manner, one can carry on one's *sādhanā*. "The universe," he says, "is within one's ownself." So giving up pursuit after external things one should realise the universal principle within one's own self; for, the Lord of the universe exists there. There will then be no difference between *in* and *out*; for these two have met in the Lord. And the perfect truth and fulfilment are to be gained only by uniting with all in spirit.

Besides this Kabīr has left many firy sayings against caste, image-worship and sectarianism. Most of these sayings are songs; for, this was the favourite form of preaching with the *bhaktas* of the Mediæval India. They have expressed themselves in poetry and music. Kabīr was not only a good composer but a good singer too.

Some of Kabīr's followers mutter the name of God with every breath. The present day *chaukā* system of the Dharamdāsī seot of Kabīr's followers reminds one of the Tāntric *chakra*. Though the *chaukā* has in it nothing objectionable yet it is a mere external formalism. It is likely that the followers of Kabīr, just like the followers of the Tantra, felt the necessity of a *chaukā* for organising a collective form of *sādhanā*. If people of common ideas do not often meet, their pursuit of the ideal may tend to grow less earnest.

Scholars like Macauliffe and Trumpp have written about Bābā Nānak, and there are among his followers some who have studied Sikhism and the life of Nānak. So in this lecture I shall touch on his life very briefly.

In 1469 Bābā Nānak was born in the village of Talbandī near Lahore. According to some *bhaktas*, Nānak was then a young man when he met the old Kabīr. On seeing him Kabīr is said to have remarked that he had no misgivings about the future; for he was seeing an able man before his leaving the world. This incident may or may not be true but Nānak was possibly much influenced by Kabīr's ideas. The central theme of many of his sayings agrees with the doctrine of Kabīr a number of whose songs have been included in the Granth Sāhib. Nānak's sayings are in Hindī with an admixture of Punjabi.

Nānak was fond of music and was himself a composer of songs. His disciple Mardānā too was a good singer. Accompanied by this Mardānā Nānak travelled extensively. Bagdad was one of the far away places that he visited.

In the place where Bābā Nānak stayed in Bagdad (about 917 A.H.) there is now a holy shrine with a Turkish inscription to commemorate the event. The descendants of Nānak's disciple of the Saiyad family are now the overseers of the shrine. All these facts together with the facsimile of the inscription have been published in the local Arabic paper of Bagdad, named the Dar-ul-Salam (9th April, 1919).

According to some authority a collection of Nānak's sayings in Arabic exists in the shrine of Nānak in Bagdad. If it proves to be true he may be called a Sūfi as well. Nānak spoke a great deal against castes, image-worship and sectarianism. The first stage in *sādhanā*, according to him, is the surrender of self in the way of love. Only one God is to be worshipped to the exclusion of all artificial things. Nānak says that a search within one's own self will reveal all sorts of valuable things. Untruth wears itself off while truth remains victorious till the end. The high esteem in which he held womanhood is revealed in this saying: "Why should you find fault with one who nourishes in her womb the leaders of men (kings)."

Mussulman *bhaktas* say that Nānak received instruction in *sādhanā* from a Mussulman *sādhaka* named Saiyad Husain but his sayings collected in the Japajī betray more leaning towards Hinduism than the sayings of Kabīr.

Nine gurus who came in successive generations that followed Nānak, fully established the Sikh religion. It was Arjun the sixth guru who collected the first Granth in 1604. After adding to this, the sayings of later gurus, the Granth Sāhib was redacted. It has been mentioned before that this work contains sayings of Rāmānanda, Nām-dev, Kabīr, Ravi-dās, Pīpā, Dhannā, Senā, Shaikh Farid and others. It contains utterances of Nānak, Aṅgad, Amar-dās, Rām-dās, Arjun, Teg Bāhādur and other gurus, and a *dohā* of the Guru Govinda. This great work begins with the Japajī composed by Nānak. Then follow all the *pads* (sayings) arranged according to *rāgs*. The same method of arrangement appears in the collection of songs or sayings of all the mediæval saints such as Dādū, Rajjab and the like.

It may be mentioned here that the Aṅgabandhu, the famous anthology collected by Rajjab for his guru Dādū, was finished at least ten years before the writing of the Granth Sāhib.

In the Granth Sāhib, after the *rāgs* come

*bhog* (offering) and *stav* (adoration) and *dohā* or collection of verses.

Every one except the Guru Govinda composed songs in the praise of Nānak. In the *bhog* section there are *pads* (songs) by Trilochan and Jaya-dev. The language of Jaya-dev's *pad* is Sanskrit with an admixture of vernacular.

To offer a resistance to the religious oppression of the Mahomedan emperors the tenth guru Govinda organised the band of Khālsā soldiers. (This Khālsā should however not be confused with the Khālsā of Dādū). Besides this he left many sayings in Braj-bhāṣā and Punjabi. After the demise of the guru Govinda his sayings were collected in 1734 by Bhāī Mani Singh. To distinguish it from the earlier work of the same name, it was called the Granth Sāhib of the tenth guru. The contents of this work are expressive more of heroism and manly courage than of spiritual attitude.

Mālik Muhammad Jāisī has already been mentioned in the first lecture. But as he was particularly influenced by Kabīr's ideas he deserves to be mentioned again in connexion with the latter saint. Jāisī's Padumāvatī was completed possibly in 1545 though the work might have been commenced in 1518. The Padumāvatī expresses the liberal religious spirit of the author. This work is much loved by *bhaktas* for the spiritual guidance it can give them. Jāisī's tomb is visited by many people even now.

We have already mentioned that the two principal sects among Kabīr's followers are the Suratgopālīs and the Dharamdāsīs. Of these the first have their head-quarters in Benares while the second in Chhattisgaṛ. Members of this second sect are scattered over different places such as the Punjab, Sindh, Gujarat, U.P., Bihar, Nepal, Sikim, and other Himalayan tracts as well as places outside India. The popularity of this sect is due to its humanism and comparative freedom from the bondage of written tradition.

Dharamdās was born in Bāṅgdhogaṛ. According to *bhaktas* the date of his birth is near about 1443. But on accepting the testimony of the Bhārat-Brāhmaṇ about his birth, this date will land us in the absurdity of finding him five years old at Kabīr's death the date of which is not disputed.

From his boyhood onward Dharam-dās was a devoted worshipper of God but in material images. It is said that in his youth he once went to Muttra where he met Kabīr who dispelled Dharam-dās's wrong ideas of God and made him settle in the love and devotion of the Supreme God. The conversation of the two has been recorded in a work named the Amar-sukh-nidhān. But according to the Ghaṭ Rāmāyaṇ Kabīr met Dharam-dās again in Benares where he convinced the latter about the futility of image-worship.

Along with Dharam-dās his wife and the eldest son Chuṛāmaṇi-dās also accepted the teachings of Kabīr. Dharam-dās was a wealthy merchant; giving away his riches he entered his spiritual career.

After Dharam-dās's death Nārāyan and Chuṛāmaṇi-dās became one after the other the chiefs of the sect. Though gurus they were married persons and were succeeded by their sons. So their sects are known as hereditary. All these have been mentioned before. The death of Dayārām Sāhib the last guru of this sect has brought the sect into great difficulties; for, he has left no issue.

Besides the two principal ones there are other sects of Kabīr. Of these the sect led by Bhaggu is to be found at Dhanaulī in Tirhut (Bihar) and the *maṭh* of the sect led by Jaggu is in Cuttack (Orissa). The Jñānī sect has its head-quarters at Majhni near Sāsārām (Bihar), while the Ṭaksārī sect is in Baroda. Nityānand, Kamalānand and Chaturbhuj were ordered by Kabīr to go for *sādhanā* to the Draviṛ country which was the native place of the Bhakti cult. It is not known whether they left any sect behind them.

Pandit Sudhākar Dvivedi was of opinion that Dādū was born of *muchī* (shoe-maker) parents in Kāśī (Benares). According to a different authority he was born in Ahmedabad (Gujarat). And his followers seek to prove that he was born of Nāgar Brāhmaṇ parents. It appears from his writings that he was a cotton-carder by profession. This information is strongly corroborated by many works such as the Jīvan-parichi (by Jana-Gopāl) and the writings of Tejānand. According to these documents Dādū was a cotton carder of the Mussulman class. At his time there were Hindu cotton-carders also, and the Mussulman cotton-carders were their converted brothers. Even after their conversion the cotton-carders remained superstitious owing to their want of education—a drawback inherited from the past. But, by his genius, *sādhanā* and association with saintly people, Dādū got over this difficult situation and developed an uncommon vision. He was quite unhampered by any burden of the past.

Dādu's earlier name was D ā ü d and the name of his wife was H a w ā (Eve). He had two sons; G a r i b-d ā s and M a s kī n-d ā s, and two daughters, N ā n ī-b ā ī and M ā t ā-b ā ī. Born in 1544 Dādū died in 1603 in Narāṇā (Rajputana) where the chief *maṭh* of his followers is situated.

Dādū had the ambition of uniting Hindus and Mussulmans as well as followers of other creeds by means of a broad ideal of fellowship. With this end in view he established his Brahma or Para-brahma Sampradāya (society). Dādū's sayings are equally deep and broad. And in these he has often paid homage to Kabīr's greatness.

Dādū who gave a high place to self-realisation had no respect for the *śāstras*. To give up vanity and to surrenderer to the One God and to look upon all people as one's own brothers and sisters was his instruction. According to him the shrine of God was within one's own self where one could meet Him only through love. One should seek union with

God through love. To make one's approach to God more intimate, instead of asking for anything from Him one should direct one's service in the course of God's service to His own creation.

Truth, which is invincible cannot be concealed in this life. After giving up impurity and evil nature one should surrender oneself to the Divine will. This leads to union (*Yoga*). One should be humble, kind, free from vanity, eager for serving others and at the same time fearless, energetic and brave. Sectarian prejudice should be shunned.

Pilgrimage, observance of vows, worship of images, rituals etc. are all in vain. One should be tolerant to all sorts of opposition and have a strong faith in God.

According to Dādū the acquisition of a guru (spiritual guide) makes *sādhanā* easy. He believed strongly in the Sahaja (natural or simple) method. His prayers are very sweet, and deep in meaning. He was, as we saw before, a house-holder and liked that others too should strive for higher life from that state.

Sayings of Dādū have been collected by his disciples Jagannāth and this collection is known under the name 'Haṛaṛe

Vāṇī'. Another disciple, Rajjab, collected his writings and divided them into 37 *aṅgas* and 27 *rāgs*. This collection goes by the name of the Aṅgabandhu. There is also another work by name of the Kāyāvelī in which also there are sayings of Dādū.

By order of Dādū, his disciples collected the writings of *sādhus* of different sects. One such collection is available with the Sādhu Śaṅkar-dās, and it was used by his guru and contains writings of sixty-eight *bhaktas* among whom there are many Mussulman names, such as Garibdās, Kāzi Kadam, Shaikh Farid, Bakhnā, Rajjab and others. Though the Granth Sāhib contains only one *pad* of Rāmānanda this collection contains no less than three of his *pads*. Besides this, there are other such collections e.g. the Sarvāṅgī by Rajjab and the Guṇagañja-nāmā by Jagannāth. Both are unique collection of sayings of Indian *sādhakas*.

Many of Dādū's disciples, such as Rajjab, Bakhnā and Wāzind Khān and others first belonged to Islam.

With Akbar the Great, Dādū had a discussion for forty days. The story goes that just after this Akbar removed his own name from his coins and in its stead printed *Jalla Julāluhu* on their one side and "*Āllāhu Akbar*" on the reverse.

The following is a list of principal disciples of Dādū:

1. Jag-jīvan—of Dyausā. 2. Sundar-dās—(Senior) was a prince of Bikanir. 3. Sundar-dās—(Junior) born in Dyausā, was a poet. 4. Kṣetra-dās. 5. Rajjab—poet and *sādhaka*, his place was in Sāṅgāner and Fatehpur. 6. Garib-dās—the eldest son of Dādū. 7. Jāisā. 8. Madho-dās—of Gular, Jodhpur. 9. Prayāg-dās—Bīhānī, lived mostly in Dīdwānā and Fatehpur. 10. Bakhnā. 11. Banwārī-dās—leader of the Uttarādhi sect. 12. Saṅkar-dās—Busherā, Jodhpur. 13. Mohan—lived often in Sāṅgāner. 14. Maskīn-dās—the youngest son of Dādū. 15. Jan-gopāl—his *maṭh* is in Āndhīgrām, Śekhāvāṭī, Jaipur. 16. Jagannāth—constant companion of Dādū and was the compiler of the Gunagañjanāmā. 17. Hari-dās—of the Nirañjan sect. 18. Niścal-dās—turned a Vedāntin later on. Each of these *bhaktas* was an outstanding personality.

Dādū's followers include many Hindus as well, though among the leaders of his sect there are many born Mussulmans. Even now, in the branch of Dādū's sect which developed under the guidance of Rajjab the place of a guru (spiritual leader) is accorded to one who is great in his spiritual achievement, and no one questions his Hindu or Mussulman birth. At Sikar, Śekhāvāṭī, Kāldairā, Bhiwānī Mālsisar in Jaypur state, at Churi in Khetrī and at Nārnaul in Pāṭiālā there are many followers and monasteries of Rajjab. Many of the *sādhus* of this sect have now become ascetics and a few of them are householders and are styled as Pandits.

Lack of time prevents quoting extensively from Rajjab's sayings; only a few are given here.

"Within our own selves is that lamp which will dispel the darkness that surrounds us."

"Can your dry asceticism vanquish the enemy that is within yourself or get any light for you?"

"In the mosque of life complete your *namāz* and salutation. It is the mind that often brings in there many distractions, so turn out the fitful mind, this kafir, from this peaceful place of worship."

"Complete your spiritual experience by developing the different sides of your life and character. The effort for spiritual experience, which in order to develop one or two aspects of life, kills all the rest is to be compared with the conduct of cats or tigers which to rear up one or two strong offsprings feed them with all the rest. The efforts of any one who develops his kindness at the cost of manliness is of the strangest kind. For it is the heroes who are commissioned to create, it is a privilege, a power which is not given to the cowards."

"There are as many sects as there are men. Such is the creation of the Providence endowed with a variety. The worship of different sects, which are like so many small streams, are moving together to meet God (Hari) who is like the ocean."

"The Ganges has come out of the feet of Nārāyaṇ (God). If in the heart of every devotee there are His feet, then the streams of ideas coming out from the heart of different devotees, are so many Ganges. The supremely holy water where all these Ganges meet can give spiritual freedom to one who bathes in it."

"Every drop of water has the call of the sea towards which it cannot start alone; for in that case it will dry up in the way. The holy stream which is formed from these drops overcomes the obstacles and dryness of the way. So bring together different streams of world's ideas and do away with poverty."

"All the world is the Vedas and the entire creation is the Koran. Vain are efforts of the Pandit and the *Kāzi* who consider a mass of dry papers to be their complete world."

"The heart of the *sādhaka* is the real paper where are written all truths in the shining letters of life. The great human world which consists of all such hearts is resplendent with the light of the complete Vedas and the Koran. Remove the obstacles of artificiality and read the truth of that world. Many are the readers of the lifeless letters written on equally lifeless paper. Read, O Rajjab if you are at all to read, the gospel which is revealed in all the lives."

The poet Sundar-dās had five principal disciples. Ṡyām-dās, Dāmodar-dās, Dayāl-dās, Nirmal-dās and Nārāyaṇ-dās. And among their followers we find many great leaders of thought and ideal.

Kabīr's teachings were no longer confined to Eastern India and through Rajputana, Punjab and Sindh they gradually reached Kaṭhiāwāṛ and Gujarat. By the time Kabīr's teachings reached Gujarat there had already developed among his followers twelve different sects such as Satya-kabīr, Nām-kabīr, Dān-kabīr, Maṅgal-kabîr, Haṅgsa-kabīr, Udā- or Udāsī-kabīr etc. Of these the Satya- or Satkabīr sect which flourished in Gujaraṭ retained much of its original liberal views, while Udā sect insisted too much on their own rules of ceremonial purity. The latter would never use utensils and kitchen used by men other than of their own sect. They would not make an exception even in case of people of their own caste or of castes known to be superior to their own. Utensils or objects or water touched by the latter cannot be used by the Udā sect who count among the followers of Kabīr.

In Surat, Baroach, Baroda and Chhota Udaipur there are many of this sect, whose children, due to this fear of polluting touch of others, cannot educate themselves in any school. It is a pity that they have lost the great ideal of Kabīr and have satisfaction in practising a perverted sort of purity which is irrationally afraid of other peoples' touch.

Bhān Sāhib (*circa* 1700-1755) was the leader of that sect of Kabīr which was working in Kathiāwāṛ with his living ideas and liberal views. He was a Lohānā by birth and migrated from Kankhiloṛ to Vārāhī. His father's name was Kalyāṇ and mother's Ambā and he belonged to the Satkabīr sect. According to Bābā Mohan-dās, Bhān was the disciple of Laulaṅgrī, a follower of Kabīr. Ambo Chhaṭṭo was another disciple of this master, and the followers of Āmbo Chhaṭṭo still exist in Dudhrej. Chief among Bhān's disciples were Kunwar, Ravi-dās, Syām-dās, Saṅkar-dās, Mādhav-dās, Charaṇ-dās, Dayāl-dās, Garib-dās, and Kriṣṇa-dās. Bhān Sāhib's son was Kṣem-dās who was famous for his spiritual attainments.

But most advanced spiritually were Bhān's disciples Jivan-dās and Trikam-dās who came from untouchable classes. Bhān had a very high opinion of these, and he said that with these disciples he would remove the miseries of his people and conquer the darkness of their heart. For this reason his followers were nicknamed as the 'Army of Bhān'.

Ravi Sāhib, another disciple of Bhān, met the master in the house of one of his creditors and found new light and life from his religious teachings. Ravi Sāhib's disciple was Morār who preached in Khambāliā, Kaṭhiāwāṛ three miles from Vanthalī station in Junāgaṛ Railway. This place is visited by pilgrims of the sect. The place of Ratan-dās another disciple of Ravi Sāhib is in Bāṅkāner. There are many of his followers mostly of mason caste. They generally visit the *maṭh* of the Rabadis and Bharwads in Dudhrej near Wāḍhwān. There are other *maṭhs* of this sect in Bāgaḍ, Māliā in Shāhpur, and Dhrāṅgdhrā.

According to many, Bhīm-bhakat was the disciple of Bhān. The disciple of the latter was Jīvan-dās who came from the Dheṛ (tanner and sweeper) caste. His place was Ghoghā-badar near Goṇḍāl. The reservoir of water in which he put hides in tanning them is held sacred by his followers. Jīvan had a disciple named Prem-dās who was Kaṛiā (mason) by birth.

Every night he walked ten miles to listen to the words of his master, which were about God, His love and our love towards Him. On being offered a boon by the master Prem-dās asked for piety and love of God. But the guru pointing out that Prem-dās has already had these two things the latter told whatever master was pleased to give might be given.

"I am childless," said the guru, "and hence my *sādhanā* will go to the posterity through your line." Prem-dās had then a daughter, and a son was born to him afterwards and the latter was the forefather of the present gurus of the sect.

Dev-pāṛā in Goṇḍāl state is the place of another J ī v a n-d ā s named B h a j a n i ā, or the singer of hymns.

The tanner Jīvan-dās had a disciple named A r j u n-d ā s—a Rajput. He too was an able *sādhaka*. Songs of these two are very popular among the *bhaktas*, and people of the locality sing them with utmost devotion.

In Bhawnagar in Kāṭhiāwāṛ there are many followers of Kabīr. But they mostly belong to the local sects.

This in brief is the ramification Kabīr's school. But through Dādū and other disciples the influence of Kabīr spread in different parts of Northern India.

Another of Kabīr's disciple, J ñ ā n i-d ā s, was the source of a few sects. Of these the M ā r g ī sect of Kāṭhiāwāṛ says that the true *sādhanā* consists in ever being in the path of *sādhanā* and there is no such thing as its cessation.

The M ū l-p a n t h ī sect was started by S ā h i b-d ā s. The Bābā-lāl sect is existent in Punjab and Mālwā its followers owe debt to Kabīr. Dārā Sikoh's interview with Bābā-lāl the promoter of this sect will be taken up later on. The Sādh sect exists in Farrukhā bād and in it Kabīr's method of *sādhanā* is followed.

In addition to these, Kabīr has inspired many more sects, such as the Saṭnāmī of Jag-jīvan, Śib-nārāyaṇis of Gāzipur, and Charaṇ-dāsis, Palṭu-sāhi-bīs, Maluk-dāsīs, Prān-nāthīs and Dariā-Sāhibīs. These sects will be dealt with later on in their proper places. We shall now take up some pre-Kabīr sects of North-Eastern India.

The Nāth and the Nirañjan cults were prevalent in Bengal and Orissa long before Kabīr flourished. The Mahimāpanth and the Kumbhīpaṭiā sect were founded later. Mukunda-dev was the founder of the latter sect which neither accepts the idol and its temple nor the sanctity of any particular caste. They are against the rule of the priest class (Brāhmans). Their dislike of the idol is so great that they are known to have once made an attempt to demolish the famous temple of Jagannāth in Orissa. Though many of their tenets resemble those of Kabīr or other *sādhakas* of Northern India it would be wrong to assume any influence of the latter upon them.

The Ananta-kulī sect of Orissa does not recognize the institution of caste. They may marry women of any caste and take their meals with any one sitting in the same row with them.

Bindu-dhārīs of Orissa observe no caste in the path of spiritual quest. They may accept discipleship of a guru from any caste. What they care for in a guru is his spiritual wealth.

On sects like the Khusi-viśvāsī, Sāhib-dhanī, Jaga-mohanī, Bala-rāmī, Neṛā, Sahajiā, Āül, Bāül, Darwesh, Shāin, Saṃjogī, Jadu-patiā and Kartābhajā etc., there have been influences of various kinds.

A great many of these came from the Sahaj, Nāth and Nirañjan *cults of Bengal* and Magadha; and a portion from Islamic sources. Besides these, it is not unlikely that teachings of Kabīr, Dādū and others of Northern India have exercised some influence on these cults of Bengal. Their history has been told by the late Akshay-kumar Dutt in his Bhāratvarṣīya Upāsak-Sampradāy or The Religious Sects of India and hence it is not necessary to speak anything of them here except the important fact that they recognize no caste, idol or scripture, and the communal idea is the most remote from them.

The early Sūfis of Sindh have been treated before and hence need not be repeated. But this does not preclude us from treating the neo-Sūfism which the Hindus and Mussulmans of U.P. and Delhi have built up. About 1600 there was in Delhi Bawrī Sāhib, a Sūfi *sādhaka*, who had a disciple named Biru Sāhib. This latter was a Hindu by birth and had for his disciple the Sūfi Yāri Shāh who flourished possibly between 1668 and 1725. Though a Mussulman by birth Yārī Shāh's sayings contain, along with the name of Āllāh, the names of Rām, Hari and tenets like those of *Dehatattva* and *Śūnya-tattva* which are connected with deep philosophical views of Hinduism; for he had none of that narrowness which may commonly be found in some Hindus or Mussulmans. In his songs we have reference to the dust of guru's feet to be applied as collyrium. Besides this, there are other beautiful expressions. "Creation," he says, "is a writing on the scroll of the infinite space (*śūnya*) with love as His pen. He who has not perceived this *rasa* within himself can scarcely be made to understand it by means of reasoning. Man is a bubble in the ocean of the Infinity."

Yāri had disciples named Bullā Sāhib, Shekhan Shāh, Hasht Muhammad Shāh and Keśav-dās. The last named flourished between 1693 and 1768. Keśav-dās's sayings called the Ami-ghūṭ or the Nectarine Drink is much loved by the *sādhakas*. He received the '*ajapā*' mantra from his master Yāri and considered himself blessed. This opened up his spiritual vision through which saw this world in a novel fashion. "The *rasa*" says Keśav, "that is longed for by crores of Brahmā and Viṣṇu, I cannot contain within myself. My eyes have opened unto God in His own form, and the wealth of beauty that I now see is too vast to be contained by this world." "*Sādhanā* means to make an end of all doubts and hesitation and lay oneself prostrate at the feet of God." Another of Yāri's disciples, Bullā Sāhib, was a Kunbī or cultivator by birth and was a contemporary of Keśav-dās. First, he was a servant in the agricultural farm of Gulāl Sāhib who later turned his disciple. Coming to know that Bullā lost himself in meditation while doing his work in the field, Gulāl became much displeased. One day he came to verify this account and found that Bullā was ploughing the field as usual, though his attention was fixed to another world. Perceiving later on, the presence of his employer, Bullā said, "you are the master of my body and it is doing its work, but my soul is with her Lord." This made Gulāl ashamed of his own conduct and the example of the Divine love and piety which he gradually witnessed in Bullā made him accept the discipleship of the latter. Bullā's many compositions, such as prayers, adoration of the *Brahman*, the description of the enjoyment of the Limitless One, and play of the liberation, are marvellous. From his writings we know that a Brāhman mendicant from the East came to his courtyard and made him intoxicated with the joy of the Absolute and with songs on the Infinite which the latter realised through the Sahaja doctrine and sung in his worship of the ultimate truth.

There is a *maṭh* in Bhurkuṛā in Gazipur in the place of his *sādhanā*.

Gulāl, the disciple of Bullā was of the same age as his guru, but he died earlier.

Born in a *zamindar* family of the Chhatri caste Gulāl was a rich man and was the owner of Basahari Tāluq in Gazipur. Though he remained a householder to the end, he gave up all pride in birth and position on the attainment of his spiritual ife. His sayings especially those containing an account of his own spiritual awakening, are very deep and sweet. His prayers and songs on the Divine love are soul-entrancing.

Besides these, his other sayings composed in the form of *ārati*, *rekhtā*, *holi*, *vasanta* are extremely popular. He has a very well-written account of the Brahma-yoga.

Another disciple of Bullā was Jagjīvan Sāhib. He wrote his Jñānprakāś in 1761. Sir George Grierson put his birth in 1682. (One Jagjīvan considered himself to be a follower of Kabīr).

He was Chandel Chhatri by caste and was born in the village of Sardahā in the district of Barābānki. He met Bullā while a boy and expressed a desire to be his disciple. As Bullā did not believe in any formal kind of initiation by muttering a *mantra* in the would be discipl's ear, nothing of that kind occurred; still his favour and potent touch changed Jag-jīvan's course of life. His soul awakened. The sect which Jag-jīvan started is called Satyanāmī or Satnāmī. His fellow-villagers going against his ways, he left his own house and removed to Kotwa two miles off from it.

He continued a householder up to the end and his daughter was married to the son of the ruling chief of Goṇḍā.

Jag-jīvan's Jñāna-prakāś, Pratham-granth and Āgam-paddhati are teachings in the form of a dialogue between the mythical divinities Śiva and his consort Pārvatī. Besides these, he has other works, such as the Prem-granth (the Book of Love) the Mahāpralay-granth the Book of the Great Annihilation). In the first of these are his prayers and discussions of *sādhanā* and in the second description of the true devotee and the true devotion.

According to him the best *sādhanā* is to attain the grace of God, and he preached the value of moral and simple life.

Knowing full well that he ran the risk of being called a visionary, he exhorted the Hindus and the Mussulmans to unite in love and spiritual efforts.

Dulam-dās, Jalālī-dās and Devi-dās were Jag-jīvan's disciples. They have some beautiful sayings. Like Kabīr Jag-jīvan too had some sayings which are riddles. His prayers are many in number.

Jag-jīvan had among his followers many members of low castes as well as some Mahomedans.

Dulam-dās, a disciple of his, hailed from the district of Rai Bareilly and his songs on purity, *sādhanā*, Divine love and grace as well as the philosophy of *ātman* are very deep.

Previous to the rise of this Satnāmī sect of Jag-jīvan there was another religious sect of the same name which stood against Aurangzeb (1672). They traced their origin to Ravi-dās and called themselves *sādhs* (=*sādhus*). This sect was again reorganized in 1750.

The sādh sect of Vīr Bhān was founded in 1658. Many of his teaching are similar to those of Kabīr and Dādū. His sayings have been collected under the title of the Ādi upadeśa probably in imitation of the Ādigranth of the Sikhs. It is divided into two parts: *Śabad* and *Śākhi*. Vīr Bhān's guru was a person who attained perfection in the realisation of the *Brahman*.

Between 1825 and 1830, a *bhakta* of Chamār class founded a new sect named Satnāmī, which became very powerful in the Chhattishgaṛ area and consisted of members of the Chamār class. These latter are mostly agricultural labourers. The centre of this sect is in Giroḍ in Raipur district; formerly Giroḍ was in Bilaspur district. In the census of 1901 their number was reckoned as four hundred thousand. Like the Satnāmīs of Jag-jīvan they avoid brinjal and have nothing to do with images and idols. The Brāhman's superiority is also rejected by them. Though Chamār themselves, they do not recognize people of so-called higher castes as their superiors. According to them real superiority consists of character, devotion and purity of conduct.

An account of the *sādhakas* of Chamār class remains incomplete if we omit the name of Lāl-beg or Lāl-gir who call themselves Alakhnāmī or Alakh-gir. 'Gir' at the end of their name is to be compared with the 'Giri' of the famous ten classes of sannyāsis created by Śaṅkara. According to the Alakh-girs their sect is older than that of Tulsīdās and they have a great influence in Bikaner. They do not worship any image and they meditate on the unseen Divinity and strive to realise Him in their lives. To them *dharma* consists in avoidance of injury to others, giving of gifts and keeping oneself pure. According to them one can attain perfect joy even in this world if one will be in the path of *sādhanā* quite forgetful of the next world. Thought of heaven or hell is fruitless, for these two things are within one's own self. One must realise by his *sādhanā* the infinite future in the living present. To enjoy complete bliss in this world by means of the *sādhanā* should be the principal object of human existence. Members of this sect do not admit the superiority of the so-called upper castes. In this respect they are quite like the Kumbhīpaṭiās of Orissa, who are not a very old sect. In reply to their want of admittance to temples they say that by entering into mean places like temples one is likely to fall from truth. *Sādhus* of this sect wear a cap and an apron made of some thick stuff, and greet each other by saying *Alakh Kaho* 'utter the name of the Unseen One'. They ask for alms in a very quiet manner and even nothing being offered they silently retire. They are respected by people as pure Yogīs of calm nature. According to them, helping others in thought, speech, service and money and in every other manner should be the duty of everyone.

The members of this sect, living in North-Western India, believe their guru Lāl-beg to be an incarnation of Śiva. They hate to be led by temptation for heaven or any future bliss, and their ideal is to realise a complete bliss in this very existence through purity, calmness and concentration of the mind. To them the present is the best part of time and their *sādhanā* aims at drinking the full cup of the present wherein the juice of great joy crushed out of Eternity will accumulate.

In about 1720 Bhikhā was born in a respectable Brāhman family in the village of Khānpur Bohanā (Āzamgaṛ). Spiritual thirst drove him to Benares, but failing to quench it there he went to Gulāl Sāhib of whom he heard in the end. With the full knowledge of the fact that Gulāl was initiated in the lines of guru born in a Mahomedan family Bhikhā received initiation from him. All this we learn from his own writings. Gulāl stayed in Bhurkuṛā where Bullā attained his spiritual perfection. After the passing away of the guru Bhikhā too remained there till his death and preached to the public.

Bhikhā's desciple was Govinda Sāhib who was an inhabitant of Ahirauli in Faizabad. Govinda's disciple was Palṭu

Sāhib. In the districts of Gāzipur and Baliā there are many earnest followers of Bhikhā. According to Bhikhā the scriptures are useless and *sādhanā* consists only of love. He says that leaving aside his pride, the *sādhaka* should be natural and simple through love, and unite himself with the universe. The entire creation is full of ideas; the day on which one realises the truth it reveals a beauty that is everywhere. On that day one feels no difference among things, and being free from a conflict between 'within' and 'without', life meets its fulfilment. His prayers and words of repentance are also very beautiful.

To some, Palṭu (*c.* 1757-1825) the disciple of (Jaya) Govinda was a second Kabīr; for his ideas have some fundamental similarity with those of Kabīr. Palṭu was born in a Bāniā family in the village Nāgpur-Jalālpur in Faizābād. He was a house-holder and his descendants still live in that very village. His co-villagers troubled and annoyed him all through life. From his writings we get some very interesting facts about the society of the time. There were at that time many vagabonds who turned *sannyāsis* for the sake of their livelihood and some of them very successfully exploited the people. Palṭu's poems in *kuṇḍaliyā* metre are very much appreciated. Some of Palṭu's sayings are as follows:

"High caste people have spoilt the low caste ones and have spoilt themselves in consequence."

"One who has seen the truth has this world for his own country."

"The truth which we see within ourselves is greater than the truth we see with our eyes."

"The *sādhaka* like a hero should have control over his passions."

"God is not the property of any particular sect."

"Do not make yourself known by your caste or creed, for that will lead to narrowness."

"Be amiable and adopt the spirit of service."

"No one can realise the truth unless he makes himself natural."

"Truth is within one's own self; to look for it in the out-side is in vain."

"One who does not see the Divinity in humanity banishes the Divinity from the natural temple."

Palṭu has many followers and all over India there are people who belong to his sect.

Though Dariā Sāhib did not make himself known as one of the Satnāmīs he called God by the name of the Truth (*Satya-nāma*). Hence it would be proper to narrate his history just after that of the Satnāmīs as well as of *bhaktas* following Jag-jīvan.

A branch of the Kṣatriya princes of Ujjain came to Jagadispur near Buxar and ruled a small kingdom there. The devotee and *sādhaka* Pīran Shāh was born in their line. According to Pandit Sudhākar Dvivedī, Pīran Shāh who was born in the line of Kṣatriya princes embraced Islam for saving his brothers from the wrath of the Mussulman Sultan. But Pīran's followers will not admit this. In a book called the Jñān-dīpak his son Dariā Sāhib has left some autobiographical touches but we do not have the above story there. Dariā was born in his maternal uncle's house in Dhārkāndhā seven miles off from Dumrāon in the district of Arrah. He passed away in 1780 and was in all likelihood born in the neighbourhood of 1700. His mother was born in a tailor's family.

From a study of the available data about his history it appears that Sūfism attracted Pīran Shāh and was the cause of his name. His son, however, was profoundly influenced by Kabīr. Dariā Sāhib married early and while still a young man he showed his spirit of devotion. At the age of thirty he began to preach. Like Mahomedans Dariā's followers sometimes offer their prayer to God in a standing posture and they call it *kornish*. Prayers which they offer sitting as the Mahomedans do, are called *sirdā* or *sizdā*. They neither obey any written scripture nor observe any vow (*vrata*), traditional custom or formalities; nor do they wear any special costume, mutter any *mantra* and make pilgrimage to any particular place. Drinking, killing any life and eating meat and fish are forbidden to them. The *sādhus* of this sect use a special kind of water-vessel called *kamaṇḍalu* or *bharukā* which resembles the *badnā* of the Mahomedans. They have four centres: Mirzapur in Chapra, Muzaffarpur, Manuwāchawki, Dañsi and Telpā.[14]

Dariā had thirty-six principal disciples among whom D i l-d ā s was the ablest. At times Dariā Sāhib went to Benares, Hardi in Arrah, and Bāisi in Gāzipur, and Magahar in Basti which was the place where Kabīr passed away.[15] Places associated with Kabīr's life were very dear to him but he never said anything to raise them to the status of holy places. Saints and devotees of Dariā's sect still speak of love, and unity of *sādhanā* between the Hindu and the Mussulman.

The Jñān-dīpak is the most cherished book of this sect. It contains beautiful songs of classical modes such as *vasanta*, *holi*, *mallār* and *behāg*. For Dariā like all other mystics of the Indian Mediæval period was a lover of music. He has also left some very beautiful prayers and songs of adoration (*vandanā*).

The history of Dariā Sāhib of Bihar should be followed by that of his namesake in Marwār. They both were contemporaries. According to his own testimony the latter was born of a (Mussulman) cotton-carder family. He lived between 1676-1758. After his father's death he was brought up in the house of his maternal grandfather K a m ī r. Kamīr lived in the village of Raṇ in Meṛtā and was a disciple of P r e m-d ā s of the village of Khiānsar in Bikānir.

The chief disciple of Dariā Sāhib Mārwāṛī was S u k h r ā m-d ā s who was a blacksmith and manufactured iron chains. It is said that B a k h t S i n g h, the Mahārājā of Mārwāṛ, was cured of his illness after listening to the ministrations of Sukh-rām.

Many consider this second Dariā to be the incarnation of Dādū. The reason of this is probably the fact that his writings are greatly influenced by Dādū and are divided into *aṅgas* (chapters) like those of the latter. But Dariā has only fifteen *aṅgas* while Dādū has no less than thirty-seven; most of Dariā's *aṅgas* possess names similar to those that occur in the Dādū's works. In Rajputana there are many *bhaktas* who are followers of Dariā, and *maṭhs* of his sect, places sanctified by the personal connection of saints of this line are widely scattered. Dariā's followers use terms like Rām, Para-Brahma and in the chapter 'Brahma-parichaya', i.e. on the Access to the *Brahman*, of the work of Dariā Sāhib we have deep ideas of Yoga. They recognize *sannyāsī* (mendicant) *sādhus* as well as those who are house-holders.

Besides Sadṇā, the butcher-saint of Sindh, there was another of his namesake born in Benares in the seventeenth century. Some consider the two as identical. Sadnā had a leaning towards Vaiṣṇavism and was in touch with Rāmānanda's school which had no faith in the Vedas, holy places and images, and denied that superiority can be attained through birth. This sect was in later times greatly influenced by sects of Kabīr and of Dādū. Their great ideal was to control senses and to attain peace, a balanced attitude and harmony of life.

Towards the close of the sixteenth century Lāl-dās was born in Rajputana among the Meos who were a notoriously predatory tribe. The majority of his followers are Meos who have a *maṭh* in the place of his birth. They practice *japa* and *kīrtan* and Lāl-dās's sayings bear marks of Dādū's influence. Kabīr too has considerable influence on him and some of Lāl-dās's sayings are strikingly similar to his.

In 1656 Dharaṇī-dās was born in the village of Mājhī in Chāprā in a Śrivāstava Kāyastha family. His father was a farmer, but Dharaṇī-dās himself was a *dewan* of the local *zamindar*.

After coming into touch with the mystic named Sevānanda, his spiritual vision unfolded. He turned a recluse and began to live very humbly in a cottage in his native village. His two works the Satya-prakāś and the Prem-prakāś are very full of Kabīr's ideas, and his *āratis* and prayers are greatly admired by the *sādhus*. Dharaṇī-dās says, "Work has value, because it is a means to realise the ideal within, in the external world. One *Khudā* (God) pervades the entire creation, human and otherwise. The Lord of one's heart does not live in a far-off region, but without any pain of longing one dose not obtain his view."

He has repeatedly emphasised the worthlessness of external things like austerities and pilgrimage. He said: "In one's life one must feel the pangs of love and have true thirst for a spiritual experience." After his demise his disciple Sadānanda became the leader of his sect.

The views and doctrines of the sects like Lāldāsī, Ghāsīdāsī and Jīvandāsī went on awakening among the masses a consciousness of the nobility of human existence. Hence came out, later on, *sādhakas* from the lower strata of society in different parts of India. It is difficult to mention them exhaustively in the limited extent of this lecture. We shall have only to select a few of them who are better known than the rest.

First, we are to mention the wellknown *bhakta* of the Punjab named Suthrāshāh. The story goes that his father deserted him on his birth because he was dirty or *kuthrā*, and Guru Har Govind picked him up and called him *suthrā* or 'the pure one'. This account seems to be quite unhistorical. The fact is that this *bhakta* was born in a Suthār or carpenter family and received his peculiar name from this fact. The original centre of the Suthrā-shāhī sect was in Barhānpur near Paṭhānkoṭe. They now have a *maṭh* near the Kashmir *darwaja* in Lahore.

But for the protection of Har Govind the deserted Suthrā-shāh might have been taken, according to law of the time, to a Mussulman orphanage. Suthrā-shāh was a great hero and gave substantial assistance to the guru Har Govind. Aurangzeb persecuted him much. But when he showed his opponents that both the *sādhanās*, Hindu as well as Mussulman, were to be found in him they stopped to persecute him.

Jhaṅgaṛ Shāh was the chief of his disciples. An annual fair takes place in the Lahore *maṭh* of the sect at the new-moon day of the month of Bhādra. Besides the one in Lahore they have another *maṭh* in Purānī Maṇḍī in Delhi. But Suthrā-shāhis of other places consider them to be almost outcastes because of their alleged contamination by the touch of Mussulmans.

The history of Pūran-bhagat who was a Yogī from his very boyhood is very popular throughout the Punjab. The centre of the followers of Pūraṇ-bhagat is at Siālkot in the Punjab. Many are the *bhaktas* who visit the place to receive inspiration for their *sādhanā*.

Garib-dās was the name of numerous *sādhakas* in different parts of India. We have already known Garib-dās the son of Dādū. Garib-dās of Chhurāṇī will be taken up later on. In the Punjab too there was one Garib-dās who was a monotheist and was in favour of uniting the *sādhanās* of the Hindus and the Mussulmans.

Chhajju-bhagat flourished in Lahore and an influence of Kabīr as well as of Sikhism is to be noticed in him. Though he was to some extent in favour of making a synthesis of the Hindu and the Mussulman ideas, yet he made some sort of compromise with the ways and manners of current Hinduism.

A thirst for spiritual life drove Bābā-lāl to Lahore, where he came in touch with Chaitanya Svāmī or Bābā Chetan. About 1590 Bābā-lāl was born in a Khetri family living in Mālwā. Though he used the name of Rām he did not mean by it any *avatār* or sectarian deity. To him *Rām*, *Hari* or *Bhagavān* meant nothing other than the One

Supreme God whom all sects ought to worship. He had faith in the teachings of Kabīr and Dādū. He says that, "Through tranquility, self-restraint, purity, kindness, service, simplicity, true vision, and by obliterating the limitation of ego, one can attain the path of *bhakti* and *prema*, which leads to the attainment of God. Love of God fills up one's being and the joy of this love-union with God cannot be expressed in words." Once somebody enquired of him about the nature of the joy available in this union of love. His answer to this was that had this joy been a matter capable of being explained by analogy there would have been no need of any striving for its attainment. To him, cessation of desires did not mean a mortification of flesh by neglecting food and clothing etc. By such cessation he understood the freeing of oneself from ignorance, error and forgetfulness about the true mission of life. God was to him an ocean of joy and an individual a drop from it. The difference between the two proceeds from the ego the individual has about the mortal frame that contains him. The cessation of this qualifying ego leads to Yoga or union. Death does not bring about this cessation for which one must have *sādhanā*.

Bābā-lāl who had Sūfi ideas also, had deep relationship with the Prince Dārā Shikoh. The various discussions on spiritual matters which the two held together have been very beautifully recorded in the Persian work named, the Nādir-un-Nikāt.

We have already referred to the history of Dārā Shikoh, but he should be mentioned once again. Many of the contemporary *sādhakas* were in touch with Dārā and were to some extent influenced by his ideals and views, and Indian *bhaktas* know him to be a *sādhaka*. Brotherhood of all religions and amity of all humanity were the objects of his great dream of life. But his premature death left his ideal unrealized. The religious catholicity among the different sects of India which he intended to develop remained an idea. Mutual jealousy among the sects which grew up later on shattered the *sādhanā* of India and the misery which came that way are yet far from being at an end.

It should not however be imagined that the difference between the Hindu and the Mahomedan *sādhanā* was the only problem that engaged the attention of Dārā. He was thinking besides how men and women, instead of being a hindrance to each other, might be co-workers in the acquisition of knowledge as well as in the path of *sādhanā.* The very brilliant group of *sādhakas* (Sūfis and *sannyāsīs*), scholars in Sanskrit, Hindī, Arabic and Persian, which met around Dārā in the Mughal palace of Delhi and discussed among other things abstruse subjects like the Vedānta and the Greek philosophy, included some ladies. In this gathering Jagannāth Miśra the celebrated author of the Rasagaṅgādhara (a work on Sanskrit poetics) recited Sanskrit poems composed by him. One of the ladies, who, from behind the screen, took part in this meeting, was a Mughal princess who was at home in Sanskrit *kāvyas* and was an admirer of the poet and scholar Jagannāth Miśra. He too cherished a love for the lady on account of her interest in him.

Once pleased with Jagannāth's poetry Dārā was ready to give him any thing he cared to ask for. Upon this the poet expressed his desire to have the princess. Dārā asked him whether the princess too was in love. The poet who was correctly informed asked Dārā to make his own enquiry. Dārā made enquiries and found out that the lady was in love with Jagannāh and said to him, "O poet, you are right and I shall fulfil my words, but the pity is that I shall lose you; you shall leave Delhi."

Dārā provided them with a horse and under the cover of night they disappeared. Arriving at Benares Jagannāth found that all the temples had been closed to him. It was enough for the people that they knew of Jagannāth's intimate relation with a woman of different faith, and they strictly avoided his contact. But of all the different sacred shrines the Ganges remained accessible to him, and it is for this reason that Jagannāth's poetical adoration of the Ganges (Gaṅgā-bhakti-taraṅgiṇī or 'the Stream of the Devotion to the Ganges) has been so very touching. Afterwards he left Benares and settled in Durgākhoh on the Ganges. In the meanwhile Dārā met his death. But Jagannāth and his wife did not long outlive him, and both of them died in Durgākhoh. Jagannāth's poem named the Bhāminī-vilāsa was an embodiment of the charms of the Mughal princess whom he took as wife.

So much about a story of human love. Dārā's dream included the co-operation of women in the intellectual and spiritual fields, and all his so-called eccentric ideas spread considerable contagion among his companions and followers as well.

At the touch of Dārā's idealism many became *sādhakas* with a very catholic and universal outlook. One of such *sādhakas* is Charaṇ-dās. Through his companions, Dārā's influence reached the sects like those of Śib-nārāyan. Charaṇ-dās did not meet Dārā but the contact with the latter's admirer, Sukhā-nanda, brought a change in the mind and life of Charaṇ-dās. And Sukhānanda was besides a follower of Kabīr.

In 1903 Charaṇ-dās[16] was born in a village named Dahrā (or Dehrā) in the Alwar State of Rajputana. He came of a Bāniā family* of Rewāṛī and was known as R a n j i t in his early life. While Ranjit was yet a boy in Dehrā his father M u r a l ī d h a r disappeared in a forest—probably fell victim to a tiger. After this sad event his maternal grand-father P r a y ā g-d ā s took him over to Delhi and began to train him for government service. But at the age of nineteen Ranjit came in contact with Sukhānanda and changed his mind for the rest of his life. At the age of thirty

According to the Miśrabandhu-vinod he was a Brāhman.

Charaṇ-dās began to preach to the people. His followers believe in the story that he received his initiation from Śukadeva Gosvāmī, the mythical narrator of the Bhāgavata Purāṇa.

Dayā-bāi and Sahajo-bāi were among Charaṇ-dās's kinsfolk. He knew them from his boyhood, and on his spiritual illumination these two ladies came to him for guidance to *sādhanā*. Charaṇ-dās set a great value on the spiritual efforts of women and gave them proper instructions.

After the death of Charaṇ-dās, Muktānand became the leader of the sect. Rāmrup a disciple of Charaṇ-dās has recorded many stories about his guru in the work named Gurubhakti-prakāśa (the Light of Devotion to the Master). His disciple Rām-sanehī was a great *bhakta* and able *sādhaka*.

The sect of Charaṇ-dās is famous for its ethical purity. Before his time many evil practices had crept into the society. Hence Charaṇ-dās's teachings did a great service to the people. He was against the following ten kinds of actions: (1) telling a lie, (2) using filthy or obscene language, (3) harsh words, (4) sophistry, (5) theft, (6) adultery, (7) killing any creature, (8) thinking harm of other people, (9) enmity to people and (10) infatuation.

The following according to Charaṇ-dās are duties that should be done: duties to family, social duties, intercourse with good people and with saintly people, devotion to one's spiritual guide and to Śrī Hari (God) who is the basis of the entire creation. Among the followers of Charaṇ-dās are two kinds of *sādhus*: house-holders and *sannyāsis* (mendicants). They wear yellow clothes. Charaṇ-dās was in favour of neat and decent dress. For the reformation of many corruptions and demoralisation of the Vallabha sect Charaṇ-dās had to struggle hard. He had the Bhagavad-gītā and the Bhāgavata etc. translated, and himself wrote works named the Sandeha-sāgar (the Sea of Doubts) and the Dharamjahāj (the Ship of Dharma). The latter is to be compared with Dārā's Shafināt-i-Auliā. His disciple Sahajo-bāi wrote works named the Sahaj-prakāś (the Revelation of Natural Truth) and the Ṣolatattva-nirṇaya (the Investigation of Sixteen Essential Truths). There are many works in the vernacular that have been written by the followers of Charaṇ-dās. Among them the Dayābodh and the V i n a y-m ā l i k ā were written by Dayā-bāi.

"This universe," says Charaṇ-dās, "is filled with the *Brahman.* The symbols like *tulasī* and *śālagrām* are useless. Good conduct and moral purity are the very first steps in the *sādhanā* and furnish its essential means. Love and devotion are its very life. But this love and devotion, expressed in other ways than in deeds, are fruitless. Practice only imparts truth to ideas." Though his ideas betray a very slight tinge of the Mādhva School, Kabīr's influence on them is paramount.

The tomb of Charaṇ-dās and the principal *maṭh* of his sect are in Delhi. An annual fair meets there during the Śrī Pañchamī. There are *maṭhs* too in Delhi and there is also a *maṭh* in Dehrā which is his birth place. But the *maṭh* which is at Bahādurpur, his paternal home, is the biggest. *Maṭhs* of this sect exist in great numbers in the Doab regions.

The Charaṇ-dāsī sect has a collection of good maxims for their daily use. One of its chapters contains passages from the U p a n i-ṣ a d s and another from the Bhāgavata. Its style is very clear and impressive.

During Charaṇ-dās's time, the political power of Islam was gradually crumbling down. The invasions of Nādir Shāh and Ābdāli, as well as the Third battle of Pānipat, occurred while he was still living. After seeing the power of Muhammad Shāh, Ahmad Shāh, Ālamgīr Shāh II pass away he died in 1782.

Charaṇ-dās had a disciple named Rāmrūp Svāmī who was an able *sādhaka*. He was born in a Gauṛa Brāhman family and lost his mother while he was three months old. As his father Mahārām did not take any care of him, a woman very kindly brought him up. From Charaṇ-dās he got his initiation in 1754. He is known as Gurubhaktānānda. His work named the Muktimārga, or the Gurubhaktiprakāśa, is full of *bhakti* for the guru and contains 2300 *ślokas*.

The Sahaj-prakāś by Sahajo-bāi is very much loved by the *bhaktas* of the Northern India. In Rajputana, the Punjab and the North-Western Province there are many *sādhus* who revere her. But had she not been initiated into spiritual life by Charaṇ-dās, she might not have realised the greatness of the latter even though belonging to the same family with him.

"Through the grace of the guru" she

writes, "I understood the value and significance of life." Much suffering came to her from her relations, but she had no complaint against them. From her writings it appears that she felt very much distressed at the ways and manners of some pseudo-*sādhus* and greedy relatives.

Dayā-bāi was another disciple of Charan-dās. It has been mentioned before that she wrote the Dayābodh and the Vinay-mālikā. Sayings of Dayā have been arranged after the manner of the collection of Dādū's sayings, The different parts contain the greatness of the guru, remembering the name of God, heroism in *sādhanā*, love, renunciation, the greatness of the *sādhus*, and *japa* along with breathing. The Vinay-mālikā contains a collection of very touching prayers by Dayā.

We have already been acquainted with the woman *bhakta* Aṇḍāl of South India and Mīrā-bāi of Rajputana. Besides these, there are other women *bhaktas* who ought to be mentioned. We shall give here a few more of their names.

Kṣemā an Ābhīr's daughter and a senior contemporary of Kabīr, was a woman *sādhaka* of very deep spiritual attainments. Conversation with this Kṣemā or Kṣemaśrī has been considered ennobling even by Kabīr. She has many very deep and beautiful sayings. Kabīr had some women disciples, of whom Gaṅgā-bāi was one. Kabīr's daughter, Kamālī, had also very deep spiritual attainments. Rāmānanda too had some women disciples. Some of their sayings are still current orally among the *sādhus*. We cannot mention them all in this short lecture. But Dādū's daughters, however, cannot remain unmentioned.

Dādū had two daughters, Nāni-bāi and Mātā-bāi. They were born between 1570 and 1575. When they grew up, Dādū gave them education and religious instruction. It is said that while living in Amber, Bhagavant Dās (Mān Siṅgh's father) the Raja of Jaypur unintentionally passed some remark on the unmarried condition of Dādū's grown up daughters; this annoyed him and he left Amber and settled in Narāṇā. Dādū wished his daughters to marry and turn householders, but they resolved to remain unmarried and devote their lives to *sādhanā*. Their words have now become very hard to procure, but a few fragments, which are still available from the mouths of *sādhus*, are very marvellously deep.

Besides the cowherd maidens of the Vraja, twenty or twenty-five other women *bhaktas* have been mentioned in the Bhaktamāl. As the Bhaktamāl is a well-known book and easily available, they may well be left out in this short lecture.

While speaking of Kabīr and his followers we have omitted the name of Maluk-dās. He was influenced more by Rāmānanda, the guru of Kabīr, than by Kabīr himself. But Maluk-dās and his disciples married and followed the life of householders. In this particular matter they have principally followed Kabīr.

In Karhā in the district of Allahabad Maluk-dās was born about 1574 (according to the Maluk-Parchayī by Suthrā-dās Kāyastha). His father's name was Sundar-dās who belonged to a Kshatri family.

From his very boyhood Maluk-dās was kind-hearted and sympathetic about other peoples' suffering. Whenever he saw a thorn badly placed in a path he removed it at once, lest this should give pain to any one. For this very soft-heartedness he attained little success in business.

Some say that he became afterwards a disciple to Viṭṭhal-dās from the Draviṛ country (Southern India). Maluk-dās as we have said before was a householder. A daughter was born to him. But neither his wife nor his daughter lived long.

He had twelve disciples, such as Lāl-dās Rām-dās, Udairām, Prabhu-dās, Sudāmā and others. After his death in 1682 his nephew Rām-sanehī become the head of his sect. *Maṭhs* and members of this sect are scattered over the entire Northern India from Bihar to Multan and even to Kābul. I have seen Maluk-dās's followers even in Rajputana and Gujarat. In Nepal too they are found.

Maluk-dās had an extraordinary faith in God. Though he has preached against the worship of images and idols, external formalism and pilgrimage to holy places, his followers are no longer immune from these. His writings named the Bhaktavatsal, Ratnakhān and Daśaratna-granth etc. are full of sayings expressing his love and devotion. Besides these there are some of his fine sayings orally carried by the *bhaktas*. Like Kabīr, Maluk-dās too taught the futility of asceticism, asked people to leave off external formalism and sectarian ostentation.

In 1717 Garib-dās was born in Chhurāṇi in the district of Rohṭak in the Punjab and in

1778 he passed away. He met Kabīr in a dream and received initiation from him at that very moment. He was a peasant born in a Jāṭh family. He was full of Kabīr's ideas. The book of devotion, which his followers study, is made up of his sayings as well as some of Kabīr's.

Garib-dās was a householder and the position of *mahant* is occupied in his sect by married people of his line.

Every year in the tenth day of the bright half of the month of Fālgun a great fair is held in the village of Chhurāni. By Garib-dās women too were initiated for *sādhanā*.

Among his disciples S a l o t j i was a very able *sādhaka*. The collection of Garib-dās's sayings has been arranged in *aṅgas* in the same manner as that of Dādū. It contains fifteen *aṅgas* and these have names similar to those of Dādū's collected sayings. The sayings of Garib-dās contain Hindu as well as Mussulman ideas and concepts. He has used terms like *Allah*, *Rām*, and *Hari* etc. According to him if one leaves aside external formalism and turns to introspection and self-realisation then only one's *sādhanā* becomes of the true kind. Garib-dās's prayers too are very touching.

In the sect of Ś i b-n ā r ā y a ṇ also

Hindu and Mussulman ideas have been blended. About 1710 Śib-nārāyaṇ was born in a Rajput family in the village of Chandrabār in the district of Baliā. He spoke very strongly against the worship of images, and was one of the pure monotheists of India. According to him God is devoid of any attribute and without any form. His followers do not use fish, meat or wine. They give emphasis on the earnost devotion to God, pure heart and character, peace, self-control and kindness to all creatures as a means to success in *sādhanā*. They recite some *mantras* at the time of bathing. People of all castes and creeds may enter this sect. A great fair of the members of this sect takes place every year in the fifth day of the bright half of the month of Māgha.

The story goes that Śibnārāyan was much influenced by the ideas of Dārā Shikoh. Some of the followers of Dārā, it is true, met him and they had associated in their *sādhanā* Hindu as well as Mussulman ideas. There are some people who believe that the Mughal Emperor Bahādur Shāh (1719-1748) was initiated in this sect. We do not know how far this was an historical fact but there is some authentic evidence of the fact that the contemporary poets like Wali Allāh, Ābru and Nāzi had great regard for Śibnārāyaṇ. He has left behind many writings, and as many as sixteen works are now available. There are many members of the Chamār and Dosād tribes who belong to this sect. There are Mussulmans and even Christians in this sect; some of the latter hail from the district of Arrah.

Bulle Shāh and Bulla Sāhib of the Satnāmīs are different persons. According to some Bulle Shāh was born in Constantinople in the year 1703. By birth he was a Saiyad and while young he felt a keen thirst for spiritual things. But he had no chance of quenching this thirst in his own native country; getting to know afterwards of Indian *sādhakas* he came on foot to the Punjab. Here he very luckily met Ināyet Shāh who was at home equally in the Hindu and Mahomedan *sādhanā*. Besides this he met some Hindu *sādhakas* too. He then settled in the village of Kasur and began his *sādhanā*.

But now the doctors of Islamic theology began to draw him into polemics because of his very out-spoken criticism of the Koran. But Bulle Shāh was more than a match for all the *maulavis* who could never defeat him with arguments. He remained a bachelor all his life and died in Kasur where his tomb still exists. Many *sādhakas* and *bhaktas* make pilgrimage to this tomb.

Bulle Shāh has left his sayings in such perfect Punjabi that one can hardly detect his foreign origin from his language. Probably this was possible owing to the fact that he came to the Punjab while very young.

The following are a few specimens of his sayings.

"People say, O Bullā, thou shouldst go inside the mosque; but of what avail will the 'inside of a mosque' be if the *namāz* (prayer) do not come from 'the inside of my heart'?".

"O Bullā, robbers reside in religious shrines, in *ṭhākur-dwārās* (Hindu temples) live the thieves and in mosques are sitting scoundrels. But God who is all love stays out of all this."

"In the mosque or in the Kaaba, in the Koran or in formal *namāz* will you find God (*Khudā*)? Whatever little I may realize by my own plain efforts gets confused when the pandits come in."

"O Bullā, there will be no liberation from a visit to Mecca, until you drive away vanity from your heart. Nor will liberation come from bathing in the Ganges though you may have hundreds of plunges in its waters.

Liberation will come only when egoism has been given up."

"O Bullā, realising Allah within myself, I have attained supreme joy and supreme peace for all time. From the daily death I have attained daily life, and daily I am going forward".

"O Bullā, remain intoxicated in the love of the Lord. Of course, hundreds of thousands of reproaches you may have for this. But do not mind them all, whenever will people say 'A *Kafir*, a *Kafir* thou art', you will only say, 'yea, yea'."

The Ram-sanehī sect was organised by the *sādhaka* Santa Ram or Rāmcharan of Rajputana. Between 1715 and 1720 he was born in the village of Sūrasen in Jaypur. In 1742 he began to preach his doctrines. Ram-sanehī means 'one who has love for Rāma' (Skt. *Rāma-snehī*). Members of this sect try to realise God through love. They do not set any value on image-worship. In Rajputana they have many *maṭhs*. Some of their *maṭhs* are also in Gujarat, Ahmedabad, Baroda, Surat, Balsar. A few years back there lived in their *maṭh* in Jodpur a great *sādhaka*, named Mahanta Dulhā-dās.

Prāṇ-nāth (1700-1750) was born in

Kāṭhīāwāṛ. After travelling over various parts of the country he settled at last in the Pānnā State in Bundelkhaṇḍ. His followers or Prāṇ-nāthīs, as they are called, are very liberal. They have equal regard for the *sādhanā* of the Hindus and the Mussulmans, and friendship between the two communities is one of the objects for which they strive. Prāṇ-nāth was equally conversant with the scriptures of the Hindus and the Mussulmans. All through his life he desired to bring about an union of the Hindus and the Mussulmans. Rājā Chhatra-shāl who met him in 1732 became his admirer. Both Hindus and Mussulmans are members of his sect. Though at home they follow their own individual traditional laws and customs, they carry on their *sādhanā* by uniting themselves at the place of their *sādhanā* by means of love, devotion and friendship. As they call God Dhām this sect is also given the name of Dhāmī. In the saying of Prāṇ-nāth terms of Islamic *sādhanā* are exceedingly plentiful.

Their means of *sādhanā* principally consist of morals, purity of character, service, kindness and doing good to others. Hindu and Mussulman members of the sect take their meals sitting together in a row. The

Kuljum, the principal scripture of this sect, is full of Hindu and Mussulman ideas. Its teachings are purely monotheistic.

Tulsī Sāhib was born about 1760. He was a Brāhman by birth, and according to some *bhaktas*, was born in the family of the Peshwas. After renouncing the world and a possibility for a princely career he settled in Hāthrās and was therefore known as Tulsī Sāhib Hāthrāsī. According to one tradition he belonged to the Āwā-panthī sect. His wife was Lakṣmī-bāi and he had a son by her. But when time came for accepting the life of political responsibility he left the word. The famous Bāji Rao II who was his younger kinsman, went to meet him at Viṭhur.

Tulsī Sāhib was at home in the essentials of Hindu as well as Mussulman scriptures and *sādhanā*. He said: "External practices and formalism are worth nothing and the real *sādhanā* is within one's own self. *Sādhanā* is nothing other than a spiritual union of the self with the world." Tulsī Sāhib delivered strong blows at the false ideas and practices of Hindus as well as Mussulmans.

Once a Brāhman while bathing in the Ganges was asking a Śudra to move off, lest his touch might pollute him. Tulsī Sāhib noticed this and said, "Yours, sir, is a very strange *śāstra*! If the Ganges is so pure on account of her origin from Viṣṇu's feet, why should Śudra who has sprung up from the self-same feet be so very impure?"

Tulsī had many *bhaktas* and other admirers. Rām-kriṣṇa the shepherd was one of them. His chief disciple was Sur-svāmī. Tulsī Sāhib died in 1842. His principal works are the Ghaṭ-Rāmāyaṇ and the Ratṇa-sāgar. His *vāṇīs* which contain many beautiful stories are very much appreciated.

We should name here the Viṣṇuite Anant-panthīs and Āpā-panthīs. The Anant-panthis are worshippers of God whom they call the *Anant* (the Limitless One). Their centres are in Rai Bereilly and Sitapur. They have their *sādhanā* in the Vaiṣṇava fashion.

Nearly two centuries ago a goldsmith named Munnā-dās of Kheri district founded the Āpā sect. This sect gives the highest place to *bhakti* (devotion) and does not set any value on castes as well as externals, such as *tilak*, *kaupin* and rosaries. Munnā-dās had no guru, and as he became a guru by his own *sādhanā* this sect is called Āpā-panth (the sect of the own self). The chief seat of the sect is in the Oudh.

Bhakta Govinda-dās founded the sect called the Govinda-panth who have their *sādhanā* after the manner of the Vaiṣṇavas. A big annual fair meet at Aharaulī in the district of Faizabad, where his tomb exists.

Bhakta Dedhrāj is one of the last great *sādhakas* of the Indian Mediæval period. In 1771 he was born in a Brāhman family in the village of Dhārsu in Nārnaul district. His father's name was Puran. Extreme poverty drove him to Agra while he was about thirteen or fourteen years of age. At that time Mādhav Rāo Sindhia was the ruler of the place. In Agra, Dedhrāj began to serve in the house of Dharam-dās who was the *dewan* of the Sindhia. In this place, he came in contact with many Hindu and Mussulman *sādhakas*. On attaining a spiritual life he began at the age of thirty-three to preach his free and liberal views. He spoke against castes and himself took a Vaiśya girl as his wife. Subsequently he went to his native place and preached his views. Nawab Najāwat Ali of Jhājhar who ruled over Nārnaul, imprisoned Dedhrāj for his heterodox opinions. He suffered much in prison but there occurring an internal trouble in Jhājhar all the prisoners were let off. After his release, Dedhrāj settled in Chhuriṇā in Khetrī and began to preach there. He died in Chhuriṇā at the age of eighty-one.

The principal centre of the sect of Dedhrāj is Bhiwānī in the district of Gurgaon. Gaṅgā-rām was a disciple of Dedhrāj and Rām Chandra was his son. I came to know Santa Rām who was his disciple. In Jhājhar, Nārnaul and Gurgaon there are *sādhakas* who are members of his sect.

According to them God is one, formless, incomparable, eternal and omnipresent. His followers do not acknowledge castes or the necessity of any image or symbol. By them, men and women are given equal place in the field of *sādhanā*. In his time, which was not modern, Dedhrāj fought against the seclusion women. Hence women of his sect do not observe purdah; at least, in their religious congregations they do not have it. At the time of prayer, their women sing and sing very well. I have seen male members (*sādhakas*) of this sect dance in ecstasy like the Baüls.

They have equal regard for the Hindu and

the Mussulman *sādhanā*. They draw out moral maxims from the Rāmāyaṇa and the Mahābhārata etc. but they do not consider these books as infallible scriptures. They refer to the Supreme Divinity by names like Rām and Hari etc. Their sayings are in the vernacular. The members of Dedhrāja's sect are also called N a ṅ g ā (naked) for the women among them do not keep themselves in purdah, and the sect is therefore called N a ṅ g i-p a n t h.

It is remarkable that Dedhrāj and his disciples, who flourished slightly before Raja R ā m-m o h a n R o y and had not the advantage of an acquaintance with the modern spirit, could stand against the castes, image-worship and an infallible scripture, and could proclaim the brotherhood of different religions and the worship of the one formless Supreme Divinity. It has been mentioned before that in their *sādhanā* they admit the equality of men and women. Their view that all men and women are brothers and sisters, because God is the common father of all, is worthy of serious consideration by all.

From now on, the m o d e r n p e r i o d of the Religious History of India began under the leadership of Rām-mohan Roy and other modern religious leaders who came after him.

I omit from these lectures any account of the Āuls, Bāūls, Darvesh, Shaīn, Saṃjogi and Kartā-bhajā etc. of Bengal, for it can well be assumed that you already know of them to some extent, and moreover time at our disposal is limited. Kartā-bhajās or the followers of the True Religion (*Satya-dharma-vādī*) include both Hindus and Mussulmans, and in this sect Brāhmans can get initiation from a guru who is born in a Mussulman family.

All over Bengal, Orissa and the outlying localities there flourished once Nāth, Nirañjan and others sects which were characterised by their very free and forcible tenets. But, for some reasons which are not clear to us, they have gradually lost their glorious position and are now begging in various ways for an accommodation however humble in orthodox Hinduism. We have no time here to discuss all this.

In the course of this lecture, we had to mention many *bhaktas* and their circles, to do justice to all of whom we require as many lectures of this length. Thus some portions of these lectures have been like a catalogue of names. But in most cases their ideals and *sādhanā* are similar, though for the sake of history we had to repeat them several times.

All of them had a desire to establish through spiritual *sādhanā* a brotherhood and a friendly unity among followers of different religions. *Sādhakas* after *sādhakas* exerted themselves for this end and they have either attained some degree of success or met failure, but a cessation of effort in this direction never occurred. Thus, to emphasise this fact we must repeat certain things, in some form or other again and again. This repetition makes clear for us the internal urge and anxiety which they felt for establishing a brotherhood among religions and unity among all people and their *sādhanā*. It seems that owing to this lofty goodwill by which the Providence has characterised her *sādhanā* India cannot find her salvation till this *sādhanā* has been accomplished. The soul of India is, as it were, changing body after body and is taking new forms as a part of its quest of salvation by this *sādhanā*. The extent of movements proceeding from this idealism and their many-sided ramifications in different places and peoples can hardly be explained without repetition. In spite of this, we have omitted from this lecture the names of those *bhaktas* around whom any sect or circle of *sādhakas* did not form after their death. Hence the careers of *sādhakas* like Kamāl or

Jñān-dās have not been discussed in these lectures. For they did not leave behind them any sect. I have mentioned here in detail only those *bhaktas* who were either followers of tradition, customs and scriptures, (*loka-veda-panthī*) or orthodox, or 'followers of truth realised by themselves' (*anbhau-sācha-panthī*) or liberal, and left behind them the tradition of their own *sādhanā*.

## NOTES

1. In pre-Vedic times long before the advent of Islam, there existed in India *prema* and *bhakti* which gradually gained acceptance among the followers of the Vedas though their rituals and ceremonies kept on playing the major part in their religious life. But on the coming of Islam the Vedic rituals and ceremonies were not only of no use, but a hindrance in the way of bringing out a synthesis of the two religions which could meet only through a revival of the very ancient *prema* and *bhakti* of India.

2. Almost all the *Ziarats* in Kashmir have been founded in old Hindu places of pilgrimage. This may also be said to have helped in bringing together Hindus and Mussulmans religiously.

3. The Padumāvatī was begun in 1518 A.C. and was completed a little before the death of Sher Shāh (1545 A.C.).

4. For reliable information about the Tantras readers are referred to writings of Arthur Avalon (J. G. Woodroffe).

5. We are giving below some important names of the Saiva and Vaiṣṇava Bhakti Schools of Southern India. Their ideas and activities will be touched later on.

Namma Āḷvār (*circa*. 100 B.C.—100 A.C.). He was the first guru of *bhaktas* like Saṭhakopa (Saḍagopa).

Tirunavukkarasu Svāmī Sundaramūrti Svāmī (700—1000 A.C.).

Mānika Vāchakar, wrote the Tiru Vāchakam (800-900 A.C.). Saiva *bhakta*.

Nanda Pariah of Chidambaram (800-1000 A.C.). Saiva *bhakta*.

Maikoṇḍadev. Organized Saivas and wrote the Ṣoḍaśa śāstra (900-1200 A.C.). *Villāla* or cultivator by caste.

Aruna Giriar (1300-1400 A.C.), son of *devadāsī*. Saiva *bhakta*. Wrote the Tiru Pughal.

Thān Mānavar (1700-1800 A.C.), a Śaiva poet of a high order.

Rāma Liṅga Svāmī-ghel (1900 A.C.) wrote the Arulpā, a collection of devotional songs.

6. The Great Master blended the canonical (*śāstrasiddha* or *vaidhī*) *bhakti* of the South with the natural (*sahaja*) and *rāgānugā bhakti* of Bengal (Gauḍa).

7. No sound conclusion can, however, be based on mere similarity of names.

8. Some more names are given in the following list:

Muktānanda (1760-1851), a disciple of Sahajānanda; in Gaṛhṛā.

Bhakta Dayārām (1776-1851), born in Dabhoi (Baroda).

Bhakta Prītam Dās (c. 1981), born and died in Devāki-gālode near Jetpur, Kāṭhiāwaṛ.

Brahmānanda (died 1831), an inhabitant of the village Sāṇ, in Dungarpur *pargana*. A Bāroṭ by caste, belonged to the Svāmī Nārāyaṇī sect.

Dhīro Bhagat (lived till 1823), an inhabitant of the village Sāwlī near Baroda.

Bāpā Bhagat (died 1844), a disciple of the preceding Bhagat. His songs give joy and inspiration to the devotees of Kāṭhiāwaṛ.

Ranachhoṛ-dās Bhagat (lived till 1724), a Bānia by birth. Preached *bhakti*.

9. It is merely believed by some that Agra-dās belonged to the Vallabha sect.

10. The Pāhuḍa-dohā, an Apabhraṃśa work, written by Muni Rāma-siṅgha who flourished about 1000 A.C., contains

some outspoken remarks about the meagre value of the *śāstras* and popular form of worshipping the Divinity. (See a review of the work by the translator in the *Indian Historical Quarterly*, vol. xi, 1935. pp. 355-356).

11. An influence of this sect is perceptible in the Jagamohani sect of Sylhet especially in the Vithaṅgal *maṭh* established by Rāma Krishna (born in 1575 A.C.) disciple of Jagamohan.

12. Historically most of these cannot be direct disciples of Rāmānanda.

13. One of the foreign critics referred to in this connection is Mr. F. E. Keaye of the Church Missionary Society, Jubbulpore. He opines that Rāmānanda did not give up idolatry though he might have criticised it. (See 'A History of Hindi Literature', Heritage of India Series, Calcutta, 1920, p. 21.)

14. A guru named Alakh Shāh from Manuā Chowki came to be associated with the Bāüls of Northern Bengal. It is for this reason that the schools of the Bāüls, Kamal Kumārī, Mājhbāṛī and Madhyamā bear more or less the marks of Pīran Shāh's influence.

15. This Magahar which stands on the other bank of the Ganges near Benares should not be confounded with the place of the same name in the district of Basti. Death in this place is free from any merit available from death in Benares.

16. There are two other *sādhakas* named Charan-dās. One of them was the author of the Bhakti-sāgar. From the autobiographical touches in the beginning of this work it appears that he belonged at first to the Rādhā-vallabhī sect of Svāmī Haridās. Another Charan-dās composed the Jñāna-svarodaya in 1480 A.C. The *sākhis* which his disciple Siddharām composed have been divided into *aṅgas* like Dādū's sayings. He has sung of the glory of guru and the Supreme *Brahman*.

# APPENDICES

APPENDIX I

## DĀDŪ'S BRAHMA SOCIETY

Dādū was religiously inclined from his boyhood. Low born though he was, he was to be found standing and listening at any place where religious discourse was being held. After he had gained personal contact with a true devotee, his one concern was: *When shall I forget my little self, my petty desires, and become established in Truth?*

Feeling Shambhar, near Jaipur, to be a suitable place, Dādū at length retired there and strove for realisation. By virtue of his fervour, free communion with the Supreme was eventually vouchsafed to him:

> "When realisation came to me, I was filled with joy and all fear departed from me. I found pure deliverance in the realm of the unapproachable, the unthinkable. The Unapproachable has come near, the message of the Unthinkable abides with me always, the Unutterable finds utterance: From separation I have *come to Union. The bonds of self are loosened, all error has fled, and the light* of the *Brahman* shines upon my soul."

He had no longer any use, says his disciple, Jangopāl-dās, for the sectarian creed of the Mussulmans, nor did he resort to any sectarian practices of the Hindus; he gave up all search for truth in the six systems of philosophy. Throughout the livelong day he remained steeped in the Divine essence, coloured with its colour. Knowing the *Brahman* alone to be the Supreme Truth, he worshipped no gods or goddesses, nor did he take to fasts, vows or pilgrimages, nor adopt the garb or sign of any religious order. To the quarrels between Hindus and Mussulmans he replied with his own life.

That, indeed, was Dādū's way. His answers to questions were given not so much by his words as by the manner of his life. And of that life one of the outstanding features was the Brahma Society founded by him. This Society grew and flourished with the expansion of its ideal, not the increase of its membership. Dādū never believed that mere addition to the number of his followers would help in gaining the truth. He was content to wait for the true devotee, whom he knew to be rare. As he says:

> "Every forest has not the sandal tree, nor is every sea full of pearls. Sages are not to be found in crowds, so also is the true devotee rare in this world."

His followers, apparently, also looked upon the formation of any separate class or order to be a danger to the truth of religion, for they always denied that Dādū was the founder of any sect. The Parabrahma-Sampradāya referred to by Dādū's disciple, Sundar-dās (though *sampradāya* means sect or cult) was this same Brahma Society, the name having been subsequently so changed to distinguish it from the well-known Brahma-sect of the Mādhvīs, from which it was entirely different. This Society was only intended to be a gathering for the adoration of the Supreme *Brahman*, who alone was acknowledged as its Guru or Head.

Their religion was often described by Dādū's disciples as *sahaj* (simple or natural). The Society itself was also sometimes called the Sahaj-sampradāya. Once, when asked by a visitor about his method, Dādū said,

> "The giving up of self-regard, the worship of God, the curing of all corruptions of mind and body, the cultivation of friendliness for all creatures,—this is its essence."

Beginning from Kabīr, many devotees of North-West India have pursued this *sahaj* or simple path of realisation, devoid of *avatār* or image, symbol or ritual. It need hardly be added that this was not the same as the vulgar offshoot of Buddhism which goes by that name in Bengal.

No two creations of God are alike, says Rajjab, the Moslem disciple of Dādū, hence there are as many sects as there are men. But, he continues, the strings of the *vīnā* each sound a different note, and yet they unite in harmonious obeisance. The individual is but a drop of the spirit, to each of whom comes the call of the Ocean of the *Brahman;* and, on the one who responds to it, is cast the duty of communicating it to the others, so that the current of devotion may flow onwards, if the individual tries to go alone to the Ocean, the arid spaces between, dry him up on the way. The love of the solitary drop is not enough, the flood of their united movement can alone overcome the obstruction of the way and, by His mercy, attain His presence.

This doubtless was also Dādū's feeling, and his friends and disciples were accordingly gathered to his side after the day's work was done. Thus a meeting place for devotees was formed at Sambhar, to which gathering Dādū at first gave no name, but simply called the place their *Alakh-darībā*, the place of the Almighty. *Darībā* means a market place, and darbā a *perch* raised on a pole for the settling of pigeons after their flight. It was perhaps the latter which Dādū had in mind in his verse:

> "The love-intoxicated devotees come to the *Alakh-daribā* to sit together in the presence of the effulgence of the Lord."

Some of his admirers used to send offerings of refreshments for the assembled devotees and, on one occasion, a poor man sent some *jawār* grain, the food of the poorest, which seems specially to have touched them, for Jangopāl-dās has recorded the incident in one of his verses. Elsewhere Dādū has likened this meeting place to a *chaugān* or park where, after the toil of the day, the devotees could forget their petty worldly concerns and come out of the narrorw limits of their own households into the fresh, open air of the Infinite. Amongst those who thus gathered round Dādū are to be found the names of all sorts and conditions of men. Of Hindu devotees there were any number, and Mussulmans also were not few. There were Kāzi Kadam, Shaikh Farid, Kāzi Muhammad, Shaikh Bahawad (also known as the Dervish), Bakhnā, Rajjab and others.

It was when he was thirty, and married, that Dādū definitely took up the formation of the Society. His disciples then began to call it the Brahma-Sampradāya, the Dādū humbly accepted the name. Later on, as we have seen, in order to avoid confusion with the Mādhvī sect of the same name, they changed it to the Para-brahma-Sampradāya. It was for the purposes of this

Society that Dādū came to compose his simple Hindī poems.

Devotees, as a rule, consider the married state to be a hindrance to realisation, but not so Kabīr, Dādū, or their followers, who looked on it as a help. Life, according to Dādū, is an immense problem, of which the solution can only be found by living it in all its departments. To attempt to reply to the vastness of the question by a narrow life is to offer it insult. *"For him who is fettered in mind all the world is a fetter. To him who is free, all worldly estates are the means of freedom. Customs and institutions keep the world in bondage and the Pandits with their confusions help them to do so."* But, loving freedom as he did, Dādū was prepared to give freedom. His two daughters, later on, would not marry, but desired to renounce the world for a life of devotion. Dādū reasoned with them; but did not press them against their inclination. The place where these two women ascetics strove for realisation is still pointed out. Women devotees frequent it and there find help and enlightenment.

Dādū with his unwavering faith in the power of the Supreme, was fearless in his up-rooting of all noxious practices, in spite of every kind of opposition from the orthodoxy of the day. He says:

> "From the day I renounced sectarianism, they were all angry with me; but, by the mercy of the Lord, I neither glory in that, nor do I regret it."

We have already noticed on a previous occasion, how when they said to him: "But, Dādū, each one follows some particular path or other, where is the example of salvation being gained by this universal path of yours, devoid of all distinctions?"—he replied:

"Great Nature itself and all great men are on my side. What cult do they pursue, earth and sky, water, and wind, day and night, sun and moon? What creed was followed by Mahomed, tell me, or by Gabriel,—to what sect did they belong? Who but Allah Himself was their Guru or Saint? The invisible God alone is the World-teacher, there is none else."

If any disciples would ask to be allowed to take the ochre garb of the ascetic he would admonish them thus:

"There are many sages and pandits, many brave and generous men, and as for ascetics they are innumerable; but those who are united to the Supreme in love are rare. If you have rejected the branches for the root, then why seek to be known by your garb? Through all the different insignia only the *self* is displayed; none of them want to take the road to God on which *self* must be cast away."

And so, in forming the Society, Dādū did not lean to any side, Hindu or Moslem. Its door was always open to all those whose faith was true, whose ideal was high, whose endeavour was earnest, whether man or woman, high or low born, rich or poor. But though some rich and influential persons did join the Society, its leading spirits were always those who could claim the greater depth of realisation. When twitted with his own low descent Dādū said:

"God is my forebear, the Creator is my kinsman, the World-guru is of my caste, I belong to the children of the Almighty."

And on behalf of his numerous low-born followers, both Hindu and Moslem, he added:

> Amongst the servants of the Lord there is neither high nor low. If the service be true, the Lord accepts it. He did not ask the caste of Sadnā (a butcher) or of Ravidās (a sweeper) but came over to them, leaving the Brāhman and the Vaiṣṇava disconsolate."

There were also slaves amongst his disciples of whom it was objected: How can these bondsmen become servants of the Lord? To which Dādū replied:

> "What of that? Is not the Lord bound by his own laws? He who has the Truth within himself cannot be subject to any other master. For the sake of the Supreme Truth, Gorakhnāth sold himself 12 times, and the gallant Āli 18 times."

At that time many of the *sanyāsis* and *faqirs* were in the habit of enticing the ignorant folk to the path of religion by a display of their magical powers. This Dādū could not tolerate. To prostitute one's spiritual power for gaining popular adherence was to him a low proceeding, an insult to the Lord. "If truth has no power of its own," was his view, "what is the use of preaching it?"

Neither did Dādū rely on any dogma, doctrine, or set forms. He had no fixed time for divine worship, in the presence of spectators. He was always rapt in the sense of the Divine Presence. When they blamed him for his lack of piety he said:

> "What is it to you, my brother, if I make no *namāz*? One should go along one's own path, and not follow that of others."

Just as Dādū did not adhere to any sect, so also had he no partiality for any particular age. He did not glorify the past, nor did he advocate any starving of the present for the sake of some future hope. Neither did he preach the subordination of courage and bravery to pity. His disciple Rajjab puts its thus:

> "The cult of pity that would kill power, and reduce manhood to impotence, is a false one. To do so would be as cruel as are the cats that kill some of their young to feed the others. A nice kind of cult, that!"

The special feature of Dādū's Society was the cultivation of all the qualities side by side,—which he called the true yoga, or coherent endeavour.

> "When all the strings of the *vīṇā* are played on, then does the melody sound entrancing. So when all the powers and faculties and ideas of man are cultivated in the same degree, in tune with the wisdom of all cults, all ages, all climes, then does it become a true yoga, the Brahma-yoga. Such is the power of true striving that all deficiencies are made complete, the bitter becomes sweet, the broken becomes whole. Such is the resulting wisdom that the very bonds become the means of freedom, the fettered are liberated, the enemy turns into friend."

If you will not form any separate sect or order, asked a faqir, then what is it you are trying to do here? Dādū said: "We are trying to make a place fit for true devotees, and also to make ourselves worthy of it." What is the sign of a true devotee? further questioned the faqir. "He who has given up his self," was the answer, is the wise devotee from whose sparkling cup priceless bliss is ever pouring out." On this the faqir came and joined them.

Dādū makes it clear that such cup is not filled with the products of the fruits of imagination, but of realisation whereof the test is peace. "He, whose mind has not ceased its struggles," he says, "has not attained true realisation."

Dādū has also illustrated this point by a story: A merchant once asked a devotee for a tireless servant. If you get such a servant, replied the devotee, will you be able to keep him supplied with work? If not, you will get into trouble. On the merchant accepting the condition, the devotee gave him a goblin for servant, warning him again that he must always be kept at work. But whatever task the merchant set him the goblin accomplished in a trice and asked for more. The merchant was at his wit's end. Whereupon the devotee rescued him from his dilemma by telling him to set up a bamboo pole and ask the goblin, whenever other work was lacking, to keep climbing up and down. That is how the merchant was saved from his goblin servant. That is how it is with the imagination. The difficulty always is to keep from running riot.

When they asked him: What is the designation of your cult? Dādū said: "Never trouble about your own designation. Your duty is to serve the Lord."

When they further pressed him: On what, then, do you seek to establish yourselves?—he rejoined:

"Who so unfortunate that he would seek to establish himself on aught else than on Him? Where else can you find a foot-hold? As the scent in the flower, the life in the veins, as everywhere the light of the sun, so is He naturally within you. He who has built this temple has not left it empty; why then would you search for other refuge? Let the lotus of the heart breathe His name, the wind of the mind carry it forth, the lips of love utter it, then will you know that the Infinite *Brahman* has entered into your life. Fear not if the way be not easy: He who is within you will fulfil all shortcomings, if but your striving be true."

Devotees, both Hindu and Moslem, found no difficulty in accepting the position of the Brahma Society, but the more obvious became the truths proclaimed by Dādū, the angrier waxed orthodoxy, till at last his friends began to caution him saying: Look here, Dādū, go a little slow. Is it good to blurt out everything before everybody? Say only what it is absolutely necessary to say,—what if sometimes you remain prudently silent? To which Dādū answered:

"Smother it as you will, truth can never be suppressed. If there be anything that is luminously manifest, whether in the depth of hell or in the height of heaven, that is Truth. The universe in multifarious ways is testifying to it, so must the devotees with their lives."

But, they urged, your truth is hurting the self-interest of so many,—the *Mullās* and the *Maulavis*, the *Pāṇḍas* and the Pandits, the *Mahants* of the monasteries and the *Pīrs* of the *dargās*. Then there are the Rajas and *Rānās*, the *Mīrs* and the *Māliks*. Day by day is their wrath roused against you. Your message to the people means the loss of their prestige and power. Bethink you well of this. But Dādū was not to be daunted. His reply to the local Raja, Bhagwanta Dās, took the form of this prayer to God:

> "O Father, I who am strong in Thy might hold *Rānā* or *Rāo* to be of no account. Thou alone art my *Mīr*, my *Mālik*, my Chief, my Lord my King; without Thee all are as thin air."

But though he was not afraid of the rich or the powerful, neither was he antagonistic to them.

> "Because I am the servant of the Lord who is the redeemer of the lost, I am happy in the company of thieves, of the breakers of law, of the scoffers against high ideals, who occupy the lowest seats with the fallen. But, though people think themselves fulfilled when in the society of their peers, how can I feel full satisfaction only in the company of my own people?"

And, as a matter of fact, his liking for such company did not stand in the way of his intercourse with even the Emperor Akbar.

There is the tradition that a messenger came from Delhi to say that the Emperor himself wished to attend the Brahma Society and accept its teaching. Dādū merely said:

> "What can the Emperor expect to gain from

this Society of poor men? But if the devotee Akbar wishes to meet us, that is another matter. He is welcome."

It is stated that Akbar appreciated the spirit of this reply and acted accordingly. In 1586 Dādū had interviews with the Emperor during a period of 40 days. This meeting should be an important landmark for students of Indian religious culture. It was from that time that Akbar had the name of God impressed on his coinage instead of his own, and promulgated the Ilāhī era.

The Kāzis and Pandits of Akbar's court, astonished at the depth of Dādū's words asked him: From what book have you got all this? Dādū answered them: "This body is my book, in which the All Merciful writes his messages. My life is my Pandit." Where is your temple, asked they, where do you pray? "My temple of God is within me," he replied, "There I worship, there no outsider can come and disturb me; bathed and clean, there I offer up my reverence."

Curious characters sometimes came to join the gathering. Once a simple Rajput youth took the vow that he would serve, without asking for any reward, the one who held the highest position. He first went to his own Raja and asked him; Do you, Sire, occupy the highest place? No, said the Raja, the Emperor is above me. Thereupon the youth went straight to Akbar and said to him: Since there is none above you I would devote myself to Your Majesty's service, asking for no return. The Emperor said: If you expect no return, why serve me? All true devotees are higher than I am. Finally the youth, hearing of Dādū from the Emperor, came to the Brahma Society's gathering and asked

Dādū: You are a true devotee; are you then above everyone else? "How can that be," replied Dādū, "when the Lord Himself is there? No one is greater than another in this place of devotion. The Lord alone is great, before Him there are no distinctions of big or small, high or low." Then, said the Rajput, I would be the servant of Him who is above all else. "Take your seat amidst us," said Dādū, "may your life be one unfaltering obeisance at the feet of the Lord!"

Dādū always maintained that realisation was only to be obtained by spiritual endeavour, by the working of the spirit within. When certain townsmen objected that they knew nothing of his spirit, but wanted to know what works he advised them to do, Dādū told them:

> "The root of all works is the realisation of Truth. Had there not been the unfailing store of snow behind, the river could never maintain its current, nor villages and towns spring up on its banks. So, for works there must be a constant fount of Truth, else their flow cannot be enduring. The spring of service is the love welling up within. Without this love the servant will tire of his service and be unable to stave off the onset of inertness. The inert creature is not even aware of the deprivation of all joy in work that overtakes him. He, whose spirit is conscious, alone tastes of this bliss. Whoso serves with love knows no weariness, he forgets his self, but cannot forget his service. Feel, consider, meditate on the evergreen earth. Ages have passed over it and yet its verdant beauty remains unsullied. What an unwearied service of love is there! Not for a day is it dulled. Why should it be,—is not love eternal life? Where love

is, there service finds its resting place. The loving Lord fills the Infinite with His presence. For Him the Earth adorns herself with foliage and flower of many a colour, the sky is filled with refreshing water, the land with resounding acclamations, keeping perpetually renewed festival in defiance of Time."

On Dādū's death his son Garīb-dās was asked to take up the leadership of the Brahma Society. After he had occupied this position for a time, he received a poem from Rajjab which began with an appreciation of him, personally: "Garīb-dās has no pride, humblest of the devotees is he; none ever turns away from him, for he is *ānanda* itself." But this was followed by a hint that his administration had its defects,—devotee as he was, he lacked proper circumspection. Whereupon Garīb-dās retired in favour of Maskīn-dās. Thereafter the gathering gradually crystallised into the Dādū-panthī sect.

It is usually the case that the principle, which first brings a band of followers together, is not maintained in its purity for long. Nevertheless the Dādū-panthīs remained true to the original ideal for over a century. The devotee Dās-ji wrote about this sect a hundred year later:

"He who has no pride, who worships the Almighty in his heart, but wears no outward sign; who has given up all men-made distinctions, who relies on no philosophy, but has conquered his own mind,—he is the true devotee, the Dādū-panthī.

He who has cast off both custom and tradition, who is not partial to any of the ten *avatārs*, but worship in his soul the One devoid of all distinctions,—he is the Dādū-panthī.

He for whom there is neither high nor low, to whom king and beggar is the same, who is immersed in the Divine Love in the depth of his heart,—he is the Dādū-panthī.

He who has conquered greed and anger and selfishness, who is satisfied with enough for food and clothing and does not keep on accumulating more and more, who accepts only alms of love and ideas, whose toil is only in the service of the world to give it gladness; whose longing and adoration is only for Him, whose only sorrow is in separation from Him, who is enveloped by the unqualified *Brahman* alone,—he is the Dādū-panthī.

He who casts away all falsehood for gaining the truth; whose thoughts fearlessly dwell only on realisation; whose words utter only the immortal truth; who, meek and humble at heart, is ever careful and clear in his judgment,—he is the Dādū-panthī.

He who is true to this ideal in word and thought and deed, he alone is the true Dādū-panthī,—the others take the name of the sect in vain."

Tripāṭhī Chandrikā-prasād, an admirer of Dādū, says:

"Because the religion of the Brahma Society, founded by Dādū-dayāl was simple and yet high, it has come to be universally honoured. Both Hindu and Moslem devotees have accepted the teaching of the good Dādū. Their worship of the unqualified *Brahman* is pure and lofty and leads its votaries to great heights of realisation. Being equally consistent with Reason and Spirit, hurting the feelings of none, it has promoted equality and fellow-feeling amongst men. It makes all men realise that they are the children of One Father, and creates brotherly and sisterly feelings. It brings mankind closer together in love, destroys all barriers between them, and helps their united advance. When it is realised that all creatures are images of the Supreme Soul, they look upon and feel for one another as themselves. They cannot admit anyone to be high or low by birth or position; they do not esteem external forms of worship, but offer up their adoration within the heart."

Even up to this day, image worship has no place amongst the Dādū-panthīs. There are several branches, both Hindu and Moslem. One of the best known of the Hindu sub-sects is the *Uttarādhi*, founded, according to Traill, by Banwāri-dās, a follower of Rajjab. Their chief centre now is in the village of Ratia in Patiala State, of which the devotee Dharam-dās was recently the head. Gopāl-dās founded a centre of this sect in Hardwar, where, of late, Sachchidānanda was a well-known figure. Sometime ago there was a movement to introduce image-worship into this sect, but owing to the strenuous opposition of the other sects, this innovation was dropped.

During these hundred years, both Hindu and Moslem were to be found among the leading Dādū-panthīs. There have been several Hindu devotees at its head who attained great heights of realisation. Among the leaders of Moslem birth were: Garīb-dās, Maskīn-dās and Faqir-dās who were all devout yogis. Even to-day, those who are member of Rajjab's branch, elect their leaders from Hindu and Moslem alike.

It will also be of interest to note, in conclusion, the impression made by Dādū's principles on some of his disciples.

Sundar-dās, who was a Vedāntin, bears testimony to the universality of Dādū's path thus:

"Whilst Hindu and Moslem were engaged in their quarrels, Dādū evolved this beautiful society of Para-brahma. What you believe in as obvious and tangible, I, by the favour of my *Guru*, have learnt to be a mere dream. The ideal he has held before us, which seems to you but a dream, is for me the only certainty. To the great teacher, now renowned as Dādū-dayāl (the kind Dādū), who looked upon men-made distinctions and institutions as so many empty names, I offer my reverent salutation."

Kṣetra-dās says:

"Neither Bhāgavata nor Śaiva, not belonging to any sect,—such was his way.

No sign not outward mark, no class name nor worldly expectation,—such was his distinction.

No injunctions of Veda or Śāstra, no symbols or practices, no rules or rigours,—such was his freedom.

No leaning towards Moslem narrowness or Hindu exclusiveness, firmly established on the Infinite, —such was my beloved Dādū!"

Jaīsā says:

"In order to saturate himself with Love, Dādū gave up philosophy and argument.

In order to understand the greatness of Man, he gave up class and clan and sect.

In order to drink freely of the beauties of Creation, he gave up the bondage of all obsessions and observances.

In order to gain the Supreme Self, he gave up himself."

APPENDIX II

## DADU'S PATH OF SERVICE

Dādū belongs to the series of Indian poet-seers,—which includes Nānak, Kabīr, Ravi-dās, Mīrā-bāi,—who were the outcome of the impact of Islam on Hinduism, and are revered by both Hindu and Moslem to this day. He was born in 1544, and died in 1603, of the Christian era. He made his living by sewing skins into bags for raising water from wells, until eventually he was initiated into the religious life by the *sādhu*, Sundar-dās. His original name, given to him by his parents, has been lost sight of; nor is there any record of the customary religious name bestowed on him by his guru. He used to call everyone "brother" and they in turn affectionately called him Dādū (pet name for elder brother) and this name of Dādū-dayāl, the good Dādū, is the one which has come down to us.*

Dādū had no book-learning, but his natural genius and the vision gained by his devotion, made him a lover of beauty and a poet. Service has its social and ethical side, expressed in the performance of civic duties and of good works. Religious fervour sometimes takes the form of rigorous discipline, or sacrifice, or penance, for their own sake. But the Path of Service which Dādū pursued was spiritual, that is to say, it was the outward manifestation of the Love of God which filled his heart.

* This explanation of Dādū's name current among some of his followers has proved to be unhistorical. For the correct interpretation of the same see p. 109.

Spiritual emotion finds its expression in works of art, in forms of ceremonial; the urgence of spiritual service finds its outlet in action, the motive force behind which is, not sense of duty, nor self-immolation, but love of God. And so its expression has all the beauty of Art, or Poetry, and is as spontaneous. Man's in-dwelling Spirit finds at least as good a medium for artistic self-expression in the life he lives, as in the paint or stone with which he works. And the spiritual devotee, like the poet or artist, finds inspiration, not in material wants seeking their satisfaction, but in his hunger after Perfection itself.

The Supreme Spirit takes form in the universe because of its joy in it. There is no compulsion of any necessity. Man attains kindred nature with God—he also is able to create artistically when he gives expression to his spiritual emotion in service, without reference to any utility, whether for himself or for others. Whenever such expression is narrowed to any purpose, Beauty does not come into being. Dādū views creation as still going on—he has no apprehension of its ever coming to an end—and for him, in the field of service, man's own creation finds eternal scope in love and joy unfathomable.

The devotees of our middle ages were none of them learned men, and they gave novel meanings of their own to the technical terms in use in our philosophy, either because they did not know their technical application, or else because they found that such application did not cover the significance of their own direct experiences.

The terms Dvaita and Advaita technically signify respectively the quality and identity of the *Brahman* and Creation. But Dādū uses these words to denote the two kinds of communion which man's self holds with the Supreme Self, the differences between which were brought out by the devotee, Ravi-dās, before him.

Man holds communion with his Divinity in two different ways. In the Dvaita, he is a supplicant, with nothing to offer, or to create for himself. Such communion is one of necessity or want, not of spiritual expansion. There the worshipper and the worshipped are at best complementary to each other, their essential spiritual unity is not recognised. Nor is such communion permanent; for, his want being satisfied, the worshipper has to come down again to his own material plane, and separation from the Divine is thus inherent in the very act of answer to prayer. In the other, the Advaita, man surrenders his self and has nothing to ask for. In the joy of mutual service the spiritual one-ness of worshipper and worshipped becomes patent. Both are creators and mingle permanently in their creation.

When woman asks for the price of her ministration, she becomes merely handmaid, losing her function of assisting in man's creation; and so in Dvaita-communion man may obtain grace as the reward of service, but not the thrill of mutual surrender. When woman knows herself as the companion of her mate, then is she mistress of her lord's heart. Then she gives, but asks not for return; and as mistress she is creator, her love fashioning her home as well as her life in its own beauty. So, likewise, in Advaita-communion, the Infinite is made manifest in the service of the worshipper; for, his service is nothing less than the realisation of the identity of his nature with the Divine. On this plane, love and joy gush forth in super-abundance, surpassing all need.

And it follows that if, in man's worship there be any narrowness, or feeling of separateness, or sectarianism,—any element of finitude, then such supreme realisation of service is obstructed. "O Dādū," deplores our Poet, "The *Brahman* in whom all separate things are to find unity,—even Him they have divided amongst their separate sects. Casting aside the living God, they have tied into bundles their own ignorance". Then again: "Each of them are ensconced in their enclosures of sect or caste, but the heart of Dādū, the servant of the Almighty, is not filled within these narrow bounds".

When they ask him: "Is it then so easy to comprehend the All in its vastness?" Dādū replies: "It rather requires overmuch intellect to maintain so many distinctions,—they are beyond my simple mind." And he adds: "Look on the Supreme Soul and you will find all souls to be one; they are different only if you cannot look beyond their differently coloured bodies. We have no eyes until we catch sight of the supreme Truth; only till then are we kept bound to sects, unable to attain the Bondless."

"But," they object, "each one follows some particular path or other; where is the example of salvation being gained by this universal path of yours, devoid of all distinctions?" Whereupon Dādū answers them: "Great nature itself, and all great men are on my side. What cult do they pursue—earth and sky, water and wind, day and night, sun and moon? What creed was followed by Muhammad, tell me, or by Gabriel? To what sect did they belong? Who but Allah himself was their Guru or Saint? The invisible God alone is the World Teacher, there is none else."

Self, according to Dādū, melts away when immersed in the depths of true Service. The good housewife lurks in the back-ground, while the household is alive and fulfilled with her loving activity. God keeps hidden away behind the veil, even in the tiniest dew-drop, but is manifest throughout the Universe in the vastness of his service. "O God", cries Dādū. "Teach me to be like Thee, mindful of service, forgetful of self. Teach me to rejoice in Thee as thou rejoicest in me, in the grand *durbar* of our communion, for ever and ever."

The worshipper he exhorts thus: "Do you hesitate, O servant, fearing that you have nothing of value to offer? Offer up yourself, in reverence, as you are: no other thought need trouble you, for that is to be like the Master. Let your striving be as is the striving of the Master, for then will your song be attuned to His. Let your service be as the service of the Master, for then will you taste of the true joy of mutual service;—not the reward of a servant, but the eternal bliss of fellowship in creation".

## APPENDIX III

# DADU AND THE MYSTERY OF FORM

The language of man has been mainly occupied with telling us about the elements into which the finite world has been analysed; nevertheless, now and again, it reveals glimpses of the world of the Infinite as well; for the spirit of man has discovered rifts in the wall of Matter. Our intellect can count the petals, classify the scent, and describe the colour of the rose, but its unity finds its expression when we rejoice in it.

The intellect at best can give us only a broken view of things. The marvellous vision of the Seer, in spite of the scoffing in which both Science and Metaphysics so often indulge, can alone make manifest to us the truth of a thing in its completeness. When we thus gain a vision of unity, we are no longer intellectually aware of detail, counting, classifying, or distinguishing—for then we have found admittance into the region of the spirit, and there we simply measure the truth of our realization by the intensity of our joy.

What is the meaning of this unutterable joy? That which we know by intellectual process is something outside ourselves. But the vision of anything in the fullness of its unity involves the realization of the unity of the self within, as well as of the relation between the two. The knowledge of the many may make us proud, but it makes us glad when our kinship with the One is brought home to us. Beauty is the name that we give to this acknowledgment of unity and of its relationship with ourselves.

It is through the beauty of Nature, or of Human Character, or Service, that we get our glimpses of the Supreme Soul whose essence is bliss. Or rather, it is when we became conscious of Him in Nature, or Art, or Service that Beauty flashes out. And whenever we thus light upon the Dweller-within, all discord disappears and Love and Beauty are seen inseparable from Truth. It is really the coming of Truth to us as kinsman which floods our being with Joy.

This realization in Joy is immediate, self-sufficient, ultimate. When the self experiences Joy within, it is completely satisfied and has nothing more to ask from the outside world. Joy, as we know it, is a direct, synthetic measure of Beauty and neither awaits nor depends upon any analytical process. In our Joy, further, we behold not only the unity, but also the origin, for the Beauty which tells us of Him can be nothing but radiance reflected, melody re-echoed, from Him; else would all this have been unmeaning indeed —Society, Civilization, Humanity. The progress of Man would otherwise have ended in an orgy of the gratification of his animal passions.

The power of realization, for each particular individual, is limited. All do not attain the privilege of directly apprehending the universal Unity. Nevertheless, a partial vision of it, say in a flower, or in a friend, is a common experience; moreover, the potentiality is inherent in every individual soul, by dint of disciplined striving, to effect its own expansion and thereupon eventually to achieve the realization of the Supreme Soul.

By whom, meanwhile, are these ineffable tidings from the realm of the Spirit, the world of the Infinite, brought to us? Not by potentates or philosophers, but by the poor, the untuotored, the despised. And with what superb assurance do they lead us out of the desert of the intellect into the paradise of the Spirit!

When our metaphysicians, dividing themselves into rival schools of Monism, Dualism or Monistic-Dualism, had joined together in dismissing the world as Māyā, then, up from the depths of their social obscurity, rose these cobblers, weavers, and sewers of bags proclaiming such theorems of the intellect to be all nonsense; for the metaphysicians had not seen with their own inner vision how the world overflowed with Truth and Love, Beauty and Joy.

Dādū, Ravi-dās, Kabīr and Nānak were not ascetics; they bore no message of poverty, or renunciation, for their own sake; they were poets who had pierced the curtain of appearances and had glimpses of the world of Unity, where God himself is a poet. Their words cannot stand the glare of logical criticism; they babble, like babes, of the joy of their vision of Him, of the ecstasy into which His music has thrown them.

Nevertheless, it is they, not the scientists or philosophers, who have taught us of reality. On the one side the Supreme Soul is alone, on the other my individual soul is alone. If the two do not come together, then indeed there befalls the greatest of all calamities, the utter emptiness of chaos. For all the abundance of His inherent joy, God is in want of my joy of Him; and Reality in its perfection only blossoms where we meet.

"When I look upon the beauty of this Universe," said Dādū, "I cannot help asking: 'How, O Lord, did you come to creat it? What sudden wave of joy coursing through your being compelled its own manifestation? Was it really due to desire for self-expression, or simply on the impulse of emotion? Or was it perhaps just your fancy to revel in the play of form? Is this play then so delightful to you; or is it that you would see your own inborn delight thus take shape?' Oh, how can these questions be answered in words?" cries Dādū. "Only those who know will understand."

"Why not go to him who has wrought this marvel," says Dādū elsewhere, "and ask: 'Cannot your own message make clear this wondrous making of the One into the many?' When I look on creation as beauty of from, I see only Form and Beauty. When I look on it as life, everywhere I see Life. When I look on it as the *Brahman*, then indeed is Dādū at a loss for words. When I see it in relation, it is of bewildering variety. When I see it in my own soul, all its variousness is merged in the beauty of the Supreme Soul. This eye of mine then becomes, also the eye of the *Brahman*, and in this exchange or mutual vision does Dādū behold Truth."

The eye cannot see the face—for that purpose a mirror is necessary. That is to say, either the face has to be put at a distance from the eye, or the eye moved away from the face—in any case what was one has to be made into two. The image is not the face itself, but how else is that to be seen?

So does God mirror Himself in Creation; and since He cannot place Himself outside His own Infinity, He can only gain a vision of Himself—and get a taste of His own joy—through my joy in Him and in His Universe. Hence the anxious striving of the devotee to keep himself thoroughly pure—not through any pride of puritanism, but because his soul is the playground where God would revel in Himself. Had not God's radiance, His beauty, thus found its form in the Universe, its joy in the devotee, He would have remained mere formless, colourless Being in the nothingness of infinity.

This is what makes the Mystery so profound, so inscrutable. Whether we say that only the *Brahman* is true, or only the universe is true, we are equally far from the Truth, which can only be expressed as both *this* and *that*, or neither *this* nor *that*.

And Dādū can only hint at it by saying: "Neither death nor life is He; He neither goes out, nor does He come in; nor sleeps, nor wakes; nor wants, nor is satisfied. He is neither I nor you, neither One or Two. For no sooner do I say that all is One, than I find us both: and when I say there are two, I see we're One. So, O Dādū, rest content to look on Him just as He is, in the deep of your heart, and give up wrestling with vain imaginings and empty words.

"Words shower", Dādū goes on, "when spouts the fount of the intellect; but where realization grows, there music has its seat." When the intellect confesses defeat, and words fail, then, indeed, from the depth of the heart wells up the song of the joy of realization. What words cannot make clear, melody can; to its strains one can revel in the vision of God in His revels.

"That is why", cries Dādū, "your universe, this creation of yours, has charmed me so—your waters and your breezes, and this earth which holds them, with its ranges of mountains, its great oceans, its snow-capped poles, its blazing sun, because, through all the three regions of earth, sky and heaven, amidst all their multifarious life, it is your ministration, your beauty, that keeps me enthralled. Who can know you, O Invisible, Unapproachable, Unfathomable! Dādū has no desire to know; he is satisfied to remain enraptured with all this beauty of yours, and to rejoice in it with you."

To look upon Form as the play of His love is not to belittle it. In creating the senses God did not intend them to be starved. "And so", says Dādū, "the eye is feasted with colour, the ear with music, the palate with flavours, wondrously provided." And we find that the body longs for the spirit, the spirit for the body; the flower for the scent, the scent for the flower; our words for truth, the Truth for words; form for its ideal; the idea for form; all thus mutual worship is but the worship of the ineffable Reality behind, by whose Presence every one of them is glorified. And Dādū struggles not, but simply keeps his heart open to this shower of love and thus rejoices in perpetual Springtime.

Every vessel of form the Formless fills with Himself, and in their beauty He gains them in return. With His love the Passionless fulfils every devoted heart and sets it a-dance, and their love streams back to the Colourless, variegated with the tints of each. Beauteous Creation yields up her charms, in all their purity, to her Lord. Need she make further protestation, in words of their mutual love? So Dādū surrenders his heart mind and soul at the feet of his Beloved. His one care is that they be not sullied.

If any one should object that evanescent Form is not worthy to represent the Eternal, Dādū would answer that it is just because Form is fleeting that it is a help, not a hindrance, to His worship. While returning, back to its Origin, it captures our mind and takes it along with itself. The call of Beauty tells us of the Unthinkable, towards whom it lies, In passing over us, Death assures us of the truth of Life.

APPENDIX IV

# BAULS AND THEIR CULT OF MAN

Bāül means madcap, from *bāyu* (Skt. *vāyu*) in its sense of nerve-current. Some try to derive the name Bāül from *bāyu* in its other meaning of air-current, on the supposition that in the cult of the Bāüls, realisation is dependant on the rousing of the spiritual forces by regulated breathing exercises. I am unable to accept this, because from the Śiva-Saṃhitā and other books we find that it is wisdom gained by meditation and concentration that is clearly laid own to be the means of realisation. Moreover the former derivation is supported by the following verse of Nara-hari:

> That is why, brother, I became a madcap Bāül.
> No master I obey, nor injunctions, canons or customs,—
> Now no men-made distinctions have any hold on me,—
> And I revel only in the gladness of my own welling love.
> In love there's no separation, but commingling always,
> So I rejoice in song and dance with each and all.

Here the term Bāül and its meaning occur together. These lines also introduce us to the main tenets of the cult. The freedom, however, that the Bāüls seek from all forms of outward compulsion, goes even further, for among such are recognised as well the compulsions exerted by our desires and antipathies. Therefore, according to this cult, in order to gain real freedom, one has first to die to the life of the world whilst still in the flesh,—for only then can one be rid of all extraneous claims. Those of the Bāüls who have Islamic leanings call such "death in life" *fanā*, a term used by the Sufis to denote union with the Supreme Being. True love, according to Bāüls, is incompatible with any kind of compulsion. Unless the bonds of necessity are overcome, liberation is out of the question. Love represents the wealth of life which is in excess of need. The idea appears to be the same as that under which the *uhchchhiṣṭa* (surplus) is exalted in the Atharva Veda (XI, 9). It should also be noted that Kabīr, Nānak and other upper Indian devotees, use the work *bāur* in the same sense of madcap, and in their verses, there are likewise numerous references to this idea of "death in life."

The Bāül cult is followed by householders as well as homeless wanderers, neither of whom acknowledge class or caste, special deities, temples or sacred places. Though they congregate on the occasion of religious festivals, mainly of the Vaiṣṇavas, held in special centres they never enter any temple. They do not set up any images of divinities, or religious symbols, in their own places of worship or mystic realisation. True, they sometimes maintain with care and reverence, spots sacred to some esteemed master or devotee, but they perform no worship there. Devotees from the lowest strata of the Hindu and Moslem communities are welcomed into their ranks,—hence the Bāüls are looked down upon by both. It is possible that their own contempt for temples had its origin in the denial of admittance therein to their low class brethren. Anyhow they have no use for *Ṭhākor-ṭhōkor* (deity or divinity), say they, What need have we of other temples,—is not this body of ours the temple where the Supreme Spirit has His abode? The human body, despised by most other religions, is thus for them the holy of holies, wherein the Divine is intimately enshrined as the *Man of the Heart*. And in this wise is the dignity of Man upheld by them.

Kabīr, Nānak, Ravi-dās, Dādū and his followers, have also called man's body the temple of God,—the microcosm in which the cosmic abode of the all-pervading Supreme Being is represented.

Kabīr says:

> In this body is the Garden of Paradise; herein are comprised the seven seas and the myriad stars; here is the Creator manifest. (I-101).
>
> In this body are the temples of the gods and all pilgrimages (I-85).

Dādū says:

> This body is my scripture; herein the All-Merciful has written for me His message. (XIII, 41).

Rajjab (Dādū's Chief Moslem disciple) says:

> Within the devotee is the paper on which the scriptures are written in letters of Life. But few care to read them; they turn a deaf ear to the message of the heart.

Most Indian sects adopt some distinct way of keeping the hairs of head and face as a sign of their sect or order. Therefore, so as to avoid being dragged into any such distinction, Bāüls allow hair and beard and moustache to grow freely. Thus do we remain simple, they say. The similar practice of the Sikhs in this matter is to be noted. Neither do the Bāüls believe that lack of clothing or bareness of body conduce to religious merit. According to them the whole body should be kept decently covered. Hence their long robe, for which if they cannot afford a new piece of cloth, they gather rags and make it of patches. In this they are different from the ascetic sanyāsins, but resemble rather the Buddhist monks.

The Bāüls do not believe in aloofness from, or renunciation of, any person or thing; their central idea is *yoga*, attachment to and communion with the divine and its manifestations. as the means of realisation. We fail to recognise the temple of God in the bodily life of man, they explain, because its lamp is not alight. The true, vision must be attained in which this temple will become manifest in each and every human body, whereupon mutual communion and worship will spontaneously arise. Truth cannot be communicated to see the divine light that shines within them, for it is your own lack of vision that makes all seem dark.

Kabīr says the same thing:

> In every abode the light doth shine: it is you who are blind that cannot see. When by dint of looking and looking you at length can discern it, the bondage of death will be torn asunder (II-33). It is because the devotee is not in communion that he says the goal is far away (II-34).

Many such similarities are to be observed between the sayings the Bāüls and those of the Upper Indian devotees of the Middle Ages, but unlike the case of the followers of the latter, the Bāüls did not become crystallised into any particular order or religious organisation. So, in the Bāüls of Bengal, there is to be found a freedom and independence of mind spirit that resists all attempt at definition. Their songs have given expression to the very heart of rural Bengal. With no claims to erudition or prestige of tradition, the spiritual heights attained by these social outcastes are yet rare even in the highest of religious orders. Their songs are unique in courage and felicity of expression. But under modern conditions, they are becoming extinct or at best holding on to external features bereft of their original speciality. It would be a great pity if no record of their achievements should be kept before their culture is lost to the world.

Though the Bāüls count amongst their following a variety of sects and castes, both Hindu and Moslem, chiefly coming from the lower social ranks, they refuse to give any other account of themselves to the questioner than that they are Bāüls. They acknowledge none of the social or religious formalities, but delight in the everchanging play of life, which cannot be expressed in mere words, but of which something may be captured in song, through the ineffable medium of rhythm and tune.

Their songs are passed on from Master to disciple, the latter when competent adding others of his own, but, as already mentioned, they are never recorded in book form. Their replies to questions are usually given by singing appropriate selections from these songs. If asked the reason why, they say: "We are like birds. We do not walk on our legs, but fly with our wings."

There was a Brāhman of Vikrampur, known as Chhaku Ṭhākur, who was the disciple of a Bāül of the Namaśudra caste (accounted one of the lowest) and hence had lost his place in his own community. When admonished to be careful about what he uttered, so as to avoid popular odium, he answered with the song:

> Let them relieve their minds by saying what will,
>
> I pursue my own simple way, fearing none at all.
>
> The Mango seed will continue to produce Mango trees, not Jambolans.
>
> This seed of mine will produce the real *me*,— all glory to my Master!

Love being the main principle according to the Bāüls, a Vaiṣṇava once asked a Bāül devotee whether he was aware of the different kinds of love as classified in the Vaiṣṇava scriptures. "What should an illiterate ignoramus like me know of the scriptures?"—was the reply. The Vaiṣṇava then offered to read and explain the text, which he proceeded to do, while the Bāül listened with such patience as he could muster. When asked for his opinion, after the reading was over, he sang:

> A goldsmith, methinks, has come into the flower garden.
> He would appraise the lotus, forsooth,
> By rubbing it on his touchstone!

Recruits from the higher castes are rare amongst the Bāüls. When any such do happen to come, they are reduced to the level of the rest. Are the lower planks of a boat of any lesser importance than the upper?—say they.

Once, in Vikrampur, I was seated on the river bank by the side of a Bāül. "Father," I asked him, "why is it that you keep no historical record of yourselves for the use of posterity?" "We follow the simple way," he replied, "and so leave no trace behind us." The tide had then ebbed, and there was but little water in the river bed. Only a few boatmen were to be seen pushing their boats along the mud. The Bāül continued: "Do the boats that sail over the flooded river leave any mark? What should these boatmen of the muddy track, urged on by their need, know of the simple way? The true endeavour is to keep oneself simply afloat in the stream of devotion that flows through the lives of devotees,—to mingle one's own devotion with theirs. There are many classes of men amongst the Bāüls, but they are all Bāüls,—they have no other achievement or history. All the streams that fall into the Ganges become the Ganges. So must we lose ourselves in the common stream, else will it cease to be living."

On another Bāül being asked why they did not follow the scriptures, "Are we dogs," he replied, "that we should lick up the leavings of others? Brave men rejoice in the out-put of their own energy, they create their own festivals. Those cowards who have not the power to rejoice in themselves, have to rely on what others have left. Afraid lest the world should lack festivals in the future, they save up the scraps left over by their predecessors for later use. They are content with glorifying their forefathers because they know not how to create for themselves."

> If you would know that Man
> Simple must be your endeavour.
> To the region of the simple must you fare.
> Pursuers of the path of man's own handiwork,
> Who follow the crowd gleaning their false leaving,—
> What news can they get of the Real?

It is hardly to be wondered at that people who think thus, should have no use for history!

We have already noticed that, like all the followers of the simple way, the Bāūls have no faith in specially sacred spots or places of pilgrimage, but that they nevertheless congregate on the occasion of religious festivals. If asked why, the Bāūl says:

> We would be within hail of the other Boatmen, to hear their calls,
> That we may make sure our boat rightly floats on the *sahaj* stream.

Not what men have said or done in the past, but the living human touch is what they find helpful. Here is a song giving their ideas about pilgrimage:

> I would not go, my heart, to Mecca or Medina,
> For behold, I ever abide by the side of my Friend!
> Mad would I become, had I dwelt afar, not knowing Him.

There's no worship in Mosque or Temple or special holy day.

At every step I have my Mecca and Kāśī, sacred is every moment.

If a Bāül is asked the age of his cult,—whether it comes before or after this one or that,—he says: "Only the artificial religions of the world are limited by time. Our *Sahaja* (simple, natural) religion is timeless, it has neither beginning nor end, it is of all time." The religion of the Upaniṣads and Purāṇas, even that of the Vedas, is according to them artificial. In this there appears to be an element of profound truth.

Bāüls who have a smattering of the scriptures say that in the first three Vedas, traces of this *Sahaja* cult of the Bāüls are specially referred to in the Vedas under the name *Nivartiya* or *Nivuttiya*, being described as those who conform to no accepted doctrines, but to whom, having known the truth in its purity, all directions are free. Not bound by prescribed rites or ceremonials, but, in active comomunion with all by virtue of their wealth of the natural, they are ever mobile. I have, as a matter of fact, found in the Atharva Veda many references to the *Vrātyas* (which may be translated as *Non-conformists*) in these identical terms. I give a few examples:

The *Vrātya* is ever mobile. He made even Prajāpati mobile (XV, 1, 1, 1).

The *Vrātya* was active in all directions (XV, 1, 2).

> The *Vrātya* went forth in all directions, and with him went all else (XV, 1. 6).
>
> Full of *rasa* (emotion), mobile and independent, the *Vrātya* entered the world, and there remained as a sea of flowing *rasa* (XV, 1, 7).
>
> The *Vrātya* went amongst men, and with him went the leaders and the assemblies, the braves and the armies (XV, 2, 1).

The Atharva is also full of enigmatic verses similar to the sayings of the Bāüls:

> The wise one who has known the *Brahman*, he alone knows the whole of language. Ordinary men use only a part of it (IX, 15, 27).
>
> There is a truth inherent in the phenomenal world, in ignorance of which the heart knows not bliss. In search of this truth do the waters ever flow (X, 7, 37).
>
> Man is a wondrous temple. When it was made, the gods came and took shelter therein (XI, 10, 18).

The Bāüls says: In the body is the essence of the world: in the world the essence of the cosmos. In the *Mahi Sūkta* of the Atharva (XII. 1) and also in several other sūktas (V. 1; VII. 1; VIII. 9; IX. 14; IX. 15; etc.), we have wonderful expressions of the mystery of creation in similar cryptic terms, which may serve to throw light on many of the Bāüls sayings.

The Bāüls claim that from the eternal *Sahaja* religion the Vedas have but called some of its truths.

But they repudiate the suggestion that it is they who are indebted for their inspiration to these scriptures; for, as they say, what have ignoramuses like them to do with scriptures? They further assert that Vasiṣṭha, Nārada and other well known Vedic seers, all pursued the mystic path of this *Sahaja* religion that permeates the world, and has yielded some of its truths to each and every religious sect. When, for instance, Nityānanda joined the ranks of Chaitanya's followers, he brought into Vaiṣṇavism many of the *Sahaja* truths, for he belonged to that cult.. His son Vīrabhadra, was a Bāül. The Bāüls freely make use of texts from the first portion of the Chaitanya-Charitāmrita, the authoritative Vaiṣṇava work by Kriṣṇa-dās, an initiate of Nityānanda's branch; for, say they, though his attempt was to compose an orthodox treatise, many *Sahaja* truths crept in, such as are not to expected from a mere Vaiṣṇava.

The Vaiṣṇavas, the wandering sects of whom have a superficial resemblance to the Bāüls, have not been able to attain to their catholicity of spirit, their power of making every religion their own, and therefore despise them as lacking in proper restraint and self-respect. The latter, in turn, look down on the former as people to be pitied. "Had these Vaiṣṇavas the understanding, they would have known better," say the Bāüls. "Chaṇḍī-dās, Vidyāpati and others were good Vaiṣṇava poets simply because they had glimpses of *Sahaja* ideas,—but are their followers competent to understand their message? They took the idea of Rādhā from us, but have dragged her down to the level of their low desires. Devoid of the realisation of the simple, their minds, obsessed with the complexities of their literature, fail to do justice to the wealth they have inherited. At best they make an attempt at simplicity and naturalness in their songs and festivals, but in their lives, their temples, their religious observances, they are unable to get free of the shackles of their scriptures. They have made a jumble of love and desire, the workings of the spirit and the inclinations of the senses. They have not the courage to realise that Jagannātha, the Lord of the World, is everywhere, and that His class-destroying festival is for ever being held. So they cannot live up to the height of the words they use."

Having no faith in scriptures, the followers of the *Sahaja* cult believe only in living religious experiences. Truth, according to them, has two aspects, inert and living. Confined to itself truth has no value for man. It becomes priceless when embodied in a living personality. The conversion of the inert into living truth by the devotee, they compare to the conversion into milk by the cow of its fodder, or the conversion by the tree of dead matter into fruit. He who has this power of making truth living, is the *Guru* or Master. Such *gurus* they hold in special reverence, for the eternal and all pervading truth can only be brought to man's door by passing through his life.

The *guru* is the past, the disciple the future, and the initiation the present, according to the Bāüls. Past, present and future are thus synthesised in the communion of Master and disciple. The Master as well as the disciple have likewise two aspects. The one is spiritual (*cinmaya*) the other earthy or worldly (*mriṇmaya*). The true initiation takes place when their spiritual aspects come into mutual communion. The mere physical proximity of their worldly aspects produces no result. The woman devotee, Kṣemā, says:

> If for years and years you hold on to the earthy part (of your *guru*) leaving out the spirit,
> You will gain neither faith, nor reverence, nor wisdom.

In the Indian religious cults only one *guru* is ordinarily presupposed. The Tāntrics acknowledge two, who give respectively intellectual and spiritual initiation. But in the *Sahaja* view such limitation of the number of *gurus* results in narrowness of realisation. Dāḍū indicates this in a verse of salutation:

> Dādū first salutes the colourless Supreme Person,
> Next, as the means of understanding Him, he salutes his *guru* as divine.
> And then he transcends the bounds of salutation, by offering reverence to all devotees.

In the Chaitanya-Charitāmrita the salutations are to *gurus* in the plural. The author, Krisṇa-dās, makes his initial obeisance to his six *gurus* (p. 10). This *Sahaja* idea finds expresion in the Tantras:

> As the bee in quest of honey flits from flower to flower.
> So do thou gather wisdom by going from *guru* to *guru*. (Kulārṇava, 13, 132).

The Bāül puts it thus:

> By what path comest thou, O *Guru*, the mystery I cannot solve,

So it passeth my understanding where to leave
my obeisance.

According to the Bāūls, initiation is a life-long process, to be gained little by little, from all kinds of *gurus*. On the occasion of one of their festivals a friend of mine happened to ask a Bāūl about his *guru*, to which he received this characteristic reply:

Wouldst thou make obeisance to thy *guru*, my
heart?

He is there at every step, on each side of thy
path,—for numberless are thy *gurus*.

To which of them, then, wouldst thou make
obeisance, my heart?

The welcome offered to thee is thy *guru*, the
agony inflicted on thee is thy *guru*,

Every wrench at thy heart-strings is thy *guru*,
that maketh the tears to flow.

My baffled friend tried again by asking the same Bāūl from whom he first received initiation. Then came the song:

The day I was born I received my first
initiation,

With one-syllabled *mantra* I begged my
mother's grace.

The tears of a mother, the milk of a mother,
my life from my mother,

And withal my mother's training I received.

Not a breath have I drawn but I gained
initiation,—that's my firm conviction.

The conclusion to which they come is that the *guru* is within.

> The *guru* who is the fount of wisdom resides
> in thine own home.
> A great mistake hast thou made by giving heed
> to the teachings of all the world.

And again:

> The voice from the depths tells thee that the
> *guru* is in the lotus of the heart.
> O distraught! Cease from thy turmoil,—
> there the darkness-killing light doth shine.

So also Kabīr:

> The Supreme Self, the *Guru*, abideth near
> to thee,
> Awake, awake, O my heart. (II, 20).

Not that the Bāüls do not admit any outward *guru*, but he is a danger to be feared, they feel, as well as a help to be sought; for, if he imposes himself on his disciple, he kills the latter's own spirit,—a murder worse than the killing of the body.

> The lamp gives light from afar, still further
> away the sun.
> The *guru* gives light without heat who sits
> aloof in the truth.

So, say the Bāüls, the *guru* should minister to his disciple from his distance:

> The bird fosters its young under its wing, the
> fish keeps its fry at its side,

But the turtle hatches its eggs in the sand from
afar,—this the wise *guru* well knows.

The Bāūls also call the *guru*, *śūnya* (lit. nothing, emptiness) not implying the absence of substance, but the spaciousness of freedom. The luminous expanse of the sky above means more to the sprouting seed than the material of the ground below. That *Śūnya* is not used in its negative meaning is clearly evident by its being also applied by them to the Supreme Being.

Dādū has the same conception:

What name can be given to Him who is
Nothing?
Whatever name we use is less than the Truth
(XIII. 145).

And again:

In *Śūnya* doth the *Brahman*, the formless, the
colourless, abide.
And Dādū has beheld, bewildered, the dazzling
light that is there. (IV. 130).

Sundar-dās has used the term *Śūnya* in the sense of the Supreme Peace in which the devotee loses himself.

The Bāūls say that emptiness of time and space is required for a play-ground. That is why God has preserved an emptiness in the heart of man, for the sake of His own play of Love. Therefore the *guru* who is *śūnya* "fosters but pesters not." So far for the mystic theory. In practice, as we have seen, the Bāūls pay high reverence to their *gurus*.

Our wise and learned ones were content with finding in the *Brahman* the *tat* (lit. that,—the ultimate substance). The *Bāūls*, not being Pandits, do not profess to understand all this to do about *that-ness*, they want a Person. So their God is the Man of the Heart (*maner mānuṣ*) sometimes simply the Man (*puruṣ*). This Man of the Heart is ever and anon lost in the turmoil of things. Whilst He is revealed within, no worldly pleasures can give satisfaction. Their sole anxiety is the finding of this Man. The Bāūl sings:

> Ah, where am I to find him, the Man of my Heart?
> Alas, since I lost Him, I wander in search of Him, Thro' lands near and far.

The agony of separation from Him cannot be mitigated for them by learning or philosophy:

> Oh these words and words, my mind would none of them,
> The Supreme Man it must and shall discover!
> So long as Him I do not see, these mists slake not my thirst.
>
> *
>
> Mad am I, for lack of that Man I madly run about,
> For his sake the world I've left; for Bishā naught else will serve.

This Bishā was a *Bhuiñ-mālī* by caste, disciple of Balā, the *Kaivarta*.

This cult of the Man is only to be found in the Vedas hidden away in the *Puruṣa-sūkta* (A. V. XIX. 6). It is more freely expressed by the Upper Indian devotees of the Middle Ages. It is all in all with the Bāūls. The God whom these illiterate outcastes seek so simply and naturally in their lives, is obscured by the accredited Religious Leaders in philosophical systems and terminology, in priestcraft and ceremonial, in institutions and temples. Hence their lament:

> Thy path, O Lord, is hidden by mosque and temple.
> Thy call I hear, but *guru* and *murshid* stop the way.
> What gives peace to my heart, sets but the world ablaze,
> The cult of the One dies in the conflict of the many,—
> Its door closed by the locks of Koran, Purān and rosary.
> Even the way of renunciation is full of tribulation, Wherefore weeps Madan in despair.

Kabīr has the following observations on this point:

> You refuse the pure water that is before you,
> Waiting to drink until you have dug a reservoir!

•

> The Smriti, daughter of the Vedas, has come to bind you in unbreakable shackles.

•

> The hedge that you put round the fields is itself exhausting their soil.

•

> Those who know all the rest have their heaven and hell,

•

> Those who know God have neither.

Dādū thus extols the followers of the simple way:

> They trouble not about Life and Death, they do not care for transmigration or cycle of existence,
> They shirk not the touch of water or wind, with Him they ever abide. (*Rāg Rāmkali, pad* 210).
> Neither confined to the home, nor wandering abroad,
> They torture not the body, but are attuned to the wise *guru's* mind. (*Gurudev aṅga*, 74).

Not satisfied with the *avatārs* (incarnations of God) mentioned in the scriptures, the Bāūl sings:

> As we look on every creature, we find each to be His *avatār*,
> What can you teach us of His ways?—in ever-new play He wondrously revels.

And Kabīr also tells us:

> All see the Eternal One, but rarely a real devotee, recognises Him. (II. 52).

A friend of mine was once much impressed by the reply of a Bāūl who was asked why his robe was not tinted with ascetic ochre:

> Can the colour show outside, unless the inside is first tinctured?
> Can the fruit attain ripe sweetness by the painting of its skin?

This aversion of the Bāūl from outward marks of distinction is also shared by the Upper Indian devotees, as we have elsewhere noticed.

The age-long controversy regarding *dvaita* (dualism) and *advaita* (monism) is readily solved by these wayfarers on the path of Love. Love is the simple striving, love the natural communion, so believe the Bāüls. "*Ever two and ever one*, of this the name is Love," say the. In love, one-ness is achieved without any loss of respective self-hood. Some of their ideas on this point are to be found in the Chaitanya-Charitāmrita, from which we cull a few stray lines:

> The follower of Love obeys neither nor scripture. (p. 720).
>
> *
>
> He who worships Krisna by the way of Love, easily tastes of his sweetness. (p. 669).
>
> *
>
> Neither wisdom nor austerity is part of Love. (p. 718).
>
> *
>
> Love seeks to please God; desire seeks to please oneself. (p. 101).
>
> *
>
> Not for me the cheap love dependent on riches. (p. 71).
>
> *
>
> He who glorifies Me and despises himself,—Me he captures not with such love. (p. 71).
>
> *
>
> I give the name of love to that which has the two-fold aspect:
>
> The love accompanying the right of possession, the love free of all ties. (p. 76).

The last idea occurs thus in Dādū:

> The body is for the world: the dweller within it for God. (XVIII. 27).

The Bāüls also have their own ideas in regard to the love of man for woman. Being asked whether he had experienced such love, a Bāül replied: "I once had a wife, my son, and for ten years or more my body was by her side. Then she departed from this world. It was ten or more years after that when, suddenly, for a moment, I knew her for the first time. And at her loving touch I became as gold."

The Chaitanya-Charitāmrita, has the verse:

> In mutual attraction they came together. leaving all else,
> But their union may or may not be, save by the grace of God. (p. 72).

Naturally the Bāüls do not look upon the love of woman as something to fight shy of, but rather as the greatest of helps to spiritual realisation. Space compels me to restrict myself to a bare outline of their doctrines in this connection.

They compare woman to a flame, of which the heat is for the use of the household itself, but the light shines far and wide. The first is called her *vigraha* (formal) aspect and the latter her *āgraha* (ideal) aspect. In the former she belongs to husband and home, in the latter she is capable of energising all and sundry. He who deals with her exclusively in the first aspect, insults her womanhood in its fulness. The internal enemies that obstruct the complete vision of her are man's lust, distraction and egotism.

The idea of *Parakīyā* (the woman not belonging to oneself) has been woeful misunderstood. The Bāüls look upon the knowledge of self as a door to divine realisation or liberation. But one's self cannot be truly known unless it becomes manifest through the love of another. Even God the Omniscient knows not His own bliss, and so seeks to discover it through the love of His creatures (symbolised by Rādhā in the Vaiṣṇava Scriptures). So is the love of a woman, who is under no social compulsion, appreciated by the *Sahajiās* as a means of man's self-knowledge and liberation. The idea has unfortunately been degraded by being understood in some quarters as a plea for promiscuous love between the sexes.

Then come the terms *eka-rasa* (the emotion that unites) and *sama-rasa* (the harmony of emotions). Space is overcome by the motion of the body; time by the course of life. And all gulfs can be bridged by the spiritual process of *sama-rasa*. If *Śiva* and *Śakti*, wisdom and devotion, remain apart, they cannot function to any purpose. "When *Śiva* and *Śakti* are united, then results *sama-rasa*."

Kabīr says:

When Love and Renunciation flow together, like
 the Ganges and Jamunā,
That alone is the sacred bathing place which can
 give the boon of *prayāga** (supreme union).
 (II. 62).

Says the *Bāūl*:

While Śiva and Śakti remain apart
The right and left streams (*of reason and of feeling*)
 remain apart likewise.
Then reason is useless, all is emptiness, and
 liberation hopeless.

*The pilgrimage (*lit.* bathing place) at the confluence of the Ganges and the Jumna is called *Prayāga*.

Listen, O Mādhā, says Jagā,

Penances and formulas, fasting and pilgrimage, reading and learning all are then futile.

If thou wouldst gain the supreme end, get the different streams to mingle.

*Sama-rasa*, with its equivalent *eka-rasa*, is therefore, obviously another name for love. It is the outflowing joy of love that alone can serve to synthesise the several one-sided endeavours of man. "It is only by this *sahaja* (simple) way," says Sundar-dās, "that man's life can be attuned to the Divine song." And as we have already shown, this *sahaja* way of love is the one that has been followed and advised by all the Indian mystics.

*Trikāla-yoga* (harmony between past, present and future) is another important doctrine of this cult. Life itself is the regulation of the activity of the present in accordance with both past and future. Kabīr once admonished an irreverent learned person thus: "Your life is an expensive bridge of marble, but it has failed to touch both banks," the implication being that he was sacrificing the future to the present.

You have devoured the three "times" (*past, present and future*) all at one time

To what end, O miserable one, have you allowed yourself to come to this pass?

You have bartered away the golden key, how will you now enter the treasure-house?—

How gain your inmost self?

O wretched one, you bring your fate on yourself!
Great opportunities had you, my heart,
But you let them slip with overmuch neglect.
Yours is now the wondrous store-house,

The folly of allowing the material interests of the present to stunt the future growth of the spiritual life becomes apparent when it is too late,—when those interests have flagged with the waning physical desires, but the wasted spiritual powers can no longer be recovered.

The same need exists for the reconcilement of the antagonism between the outer call of the material world and the inner call of the spiritual world, as for the realisation of the mutual love of the individual and Supreme self. It is a case for the application of the same *sama-rasa*. The God who is Love, say the Bāüls, can alone serve to turn the currents of the within and the without in one and the same direction.

Kabīr says:

If we say He is only within, then the whole Universe is shamed. If we say He is only without, then that is false. He whose feet rest alike on the sentient and on the inert, fills the gap between the inner and the outer worlds. (I. 104).

The inter-relations of man's body and the Universe have to be realised by spiritual endeavour. Such endeavour is called *Kāyā-Sādhana* (Realisation through the body). There are numberless instances in the poems of Dādū where the body has been eulogised as the seat of the Almighty, the pilgrimage of pilgrimages, the sacred place of worship, of realisation, and of final liberation. One of the recognised methods of attaining this realisation, is the use of the rhythm of breathing as a rosary for meditation, in place of the usual beads. This process of inhaling and exhaling the outer atmosphere, is called *ajapā-japa* as distinguished from *japa* (the telling of beads). The anthropomorphic narrowing of the Infinite Spirit of the Universe by inviting Him into the confines of the body has, however, to be guarded against. The endeavour should rather consist in the expansion of one's own self into the universe by means of the cultivation of *sama-rasa*.

Another process in this *Kāyā-sādhana* of the Bāüls is known as *Urdha-srota* (the elevation of the current). Waters flow downwards according to the ordinary physical law. But with the advent of Life the process is reversed. When the living seed sprouts the juices are drawn upwards, and on the elevation that such flow can attain depends the height of the tree. It is the same in the life of man. His desires ordinarily flow downward towards animality. The endeavour of the expanding spirit is to turn their current upwards towards the light. The currents of *jīva* (animal life) must be converted into the current of *Śiva* (God life). The former centre round the ego, they must be raised by the force of love.

Says Dādū's daughter, Nāni-bāi:

How is the divine to conquer the carnal,—
The downward current to be upwards turned?
As when the wick is lighted the oil doth upwards flow,
so simply is destroyed the thirst of the body.

The Yoga-vāśiṣṭha tells us:

Uncleansed desires bind to the world, purified desires give liberation (I. 3. 11.).

References to this reversal of current are also to be found in the Atharva Veda (X, 2, 9; 2, 34). This reversal is otherwise considered by Indian devotees as the conversion of the *sthūla* (gross) into the *sūkṣma* (fine).

The Bāül sings:

Love is my golden touch,—it turns desire into service;
Earth seeks to become Heaven, man to become God.

Another aspect of the idea of reversal has been put thus by Rabindranath in his Broken Ties:

> If I keep going in the same direction along which He comes to me, then I shall be going further and further away from Him. If I proceed in the opposite direction, then only can we meet. He loves form, so He is continually descending towards form. We cannot live by form alone, so we must ascend towards His formlessness. He is free, so his play is within bond. We are bound, so we find our joy in freedom. All our sorrow is, because we cannot understand this. He who sings, proceeds from his joy to the tune; he who hears, from the tune to joy. One comes from freedom into bondage, the other goes from bondage into freedom; only thus can they have their communion. He sings and we hear. He ties the bonds as He sings to us, we untie them as we listen to Him.

This idea also occurs in our devotees of the Middle Ages.

The Yoga of the Bāüls is essentially different from that of the Tāntrics who are mainly concerned with the different methods of gaining occult and other powers for serving some end. The *Sahaja* endeavour seeks the bliss of divine union only for its own sake. Mundane desires are therefore accounted the chief obstacles in the way. But, for getting rid of them, the wise *guru*, according to the Bāūls, does not advise renunciation of the good things of the world, but the opening of the door to the higher self. Thus guided, says Kabīr:

> I close not my eyes, stop not my ears, nor torment my body. But every path I then traverse becomes a path of pilgrimage, whatever work I engage in becomes service. This simple consummation is the best. (I. 76).

*

The simple way has led its votaries easily and naturally to their living conception of Humanity.

Rajjab says:

All the world is the Veda, all creations the Korān,
Why read paper scriptures, O Rajjab, gather ever
fresh wisdom from the Universe.
The eternal wisdom shines within the concourse of
the millions of Humanity.

The Bāūl sings:

> The simple has its thirty million strings
> Whose mingled symphony ever sounds.
> Take all the creatures of the World into yourself
> Drown yourself in that eternal music.

The raising of the *Retodhārā* (seminal current) to the higher centres, the process of piercing or rousing of the *chakras* (spiritual force centres) are special esoteric doctrines of which I can only make passing mention on the present occasion.

I conclude with a few more examples of Bāūl songs, esoteric and otherwise, from amongst many others of equal interest.

By Gaṅgā-rām, *the Namaśudrā.*

Ah, the comings and goings with every breath of ours,
The *mantra* of *eka-rasa* makes them all into one.
In you are the fourteen regions, amid them is yourself,
Yet of these comings and goings naught have you understood!
Mediate on this life movement, prince of Yogis will you be,
Realising how finite and unbounded are One, as you breathe in and out.
Of all ages, then, you will count the moments, in every moment find the ages,—
The drop in the ocean the ocean in the drop.
If your endeavour be but *Sahaja*, beyond argument and cogitation,
You will taste of the nectar of *rasa*, the precious quintessence.
Blinded are you by over much journeying from bourne to bourne,

O Gangā-rām, be simple! Then alone will vanish
all your doubts.

*

Past the seven seas, across the eight mountains
You will come to the essential principle.
From *pātāl** then you will mount the sky,
To descent again on the regions below.
Throughout the six seasons will last your festival,
In every *kamal*† will be your play.

*

My life is the lamp afloat on the stream.
To what bourne shall it take me?

By Jagā, the *guru* of Gangārām.

Within you is the unfathomable sea, its mystery
you have not solved,
No banks or shores has it of scripture-texts or rules
or rites.
Over its bottomless, shoreless expanse nor creed nor
book will show the way.
Yet cross it you must, or fruitless will be your great
boon of human life.
Could you but open your looked door, to find your
relations with All,
If by he grace of your *guru* your obstructions be
but removed,
Then, says Jagā, would you be gloriously fulfilled.

* The nether region.

† *lit.* Lotus, used of centres of man's physical or spiritual forces.

By Balā, the *Kaivarta*.

O'erhead is the mind-ravishing blue lotus of the sky.
How dazzling shine its uncounted petals in the limitless blue.
And as the beams of nectar flash from its sky-filling vastness
The drunken mind flies into its ineffable expanse, enraptured.........
Cries Balā, O brother, but what am I to do,
For ever and anon I lose my way!

By Bishā, the disciple of Balā.

The simple Man was in the Vrindāvan of my heart,
Alas how and when I lose Him,
That now no peace I know, at home or abroad?
By meditation and telling of beads, in worship and travail,
The quest goes on for ever;
But unless the Simple Man comes of Himself,
Fruitless is it all;
For He yields not to forcefulness of striving.
Bishā's heart has understood right well
That by His own simple way alone, is its door unlocked.

"Listen, O brother man," declares Chaṇḍi-dās, "The Truth of Man is the highest of truths, there is no other truth above it."

## *NOTES TO THE APPENDIX IV*

For Dādū's sayings referred to in this paper see "*Sri Swāmī Dādū-dayāl-kī Bāṇī*," edited by Chandrikā-prasād Tripāṭhi, Ajmer 1907. And for quotation from the *Chaitanya-Charitāmrita* see the edition published by Nityaswarūp Brahmachārī from Calcutta in 1334 B.E. Texts of the songs of Bāüls have not yet been published and are with the writer. For Kabīr's sayings see *Kabīr's Poems* translated by Rabindranath Tagore and published by Macmillan.

# INDEX